Startup Mixology

Startup Mixology

Tech Cocktail's Guide to Building, Growing, and Celebrating Startup Success

Frank Gruber

WILEY

To everyone out there living with an idea and a dream, big or small. I'm hopeful you'll find the courage to start, and thankful if this book can contribute to your journey and success in some way.

CONTENTS

FOREWORD

I'm a big believer in the 10,000 hours of practice theory.

If you want to become an amazing guitar player, you need 10,000 hours of practice. If you want to become a great golfer, you need 10,000 hours of practice. And if you want to become a successful entrepreneur, you need 10,000 hours of practice.

However, the other thing you need is to make sure that you're practicing the right things. If you spend your 10,000 hours doing nothing, except playing the basic chords, you will not magically turn into the amazing guitar player you imagined at the end of that journey.

Generally, my advice to entrepreneurs boils down to a few simple things:

1. Make sure that whatever you're doing, you're doing it for the passion, and money isn't your primary motivator. Chase the vision, not the money. If you do so, the chances of making more money are much more likely to happen.

2. Be unapologetically true to yourself, both in business and in life. This principle will help you build a unique brand as well as a strong company culture.

3. Trust your gut. Sometimes your gut will be wrong, but that's part of what the 10,000 hours of practice of being an entrepreneur is all about. It's about training your gut.

In my entrepreneurial experience with LinkExchange, Zappos, *Delivering Happiness*, and now Downtown Project, I've found that there's a lot you can learn from books as well as other entrepreneurs. I wish that the book that you are now holding in your hands had existed when I was just starting out. It contains a lot of great lessons and stories that would have saved me a lot of trial and error throughout my own entrepreneurial journey.

If you're in the midst of starting your own startup, this book can serve as a great guide and roadmap for things you should be thinking about, and ultimately things that you should be practicing as you form and grow your startup.

I've known Frank and Jen from Tech Cocktail for several years now. Not only have they been on their own entrepreneurial journey, they are also in the business of being exposed to and learning from literally hundreds and hundreds of startups. You'll find tons of great advice in this book from lots of different entrepreneurs.

My advice to you is to take it all in, and then chart your own path. There will be a lot of ups and downs, but just remember that it's all part of the journey.

—**Tony Hsieh**
CEO, Zappos.com;
Author of *Delivering Happiness*;
Appreciator of llamas

PS: The time you spend reading this book will count towards your 10,000 hours of practice. ☺

INTRODUCTION

I n 2005, just weeks before Hurricane Katrina hit New Orleans, I found myself attending the WebmasterWorld's Search Conference in the Big Easy. At a loss for which sessions to attend, I randomly sat in on a session called Blogging for Fun and Profit. I had never really understood blogging. It was an unusual word, it seemed nerdy, and I didn't get its appeal, but I reluctantly stayed—vowing that I would listen but never blog.

What I didn't know was that this session and what I learned that hour from Yahoo!'s Jeremy Zawodny and PhD Amanda Watlington would be pivotal in my life's trajectory. An interesting convergence of my skills, interests, and new opportunities arose: my computer technology background from Purdue and Northwestern, my inner passion to be the captain of my own ship, my love of writing, and the knowledge that I could launch something online and grow an audience without the help of a large company. Little did I know at the time that attending this blogging session would be the aha moment I needed to launch Tech Cocktail, a tech startup-focused news and events organization, the following spring.

The next few years included jobs for large Fortune 500 companies, as well as numerous projects I "started up" during nights and weekends. From building a spam-blog-fighting tool to building a college-targeted social network that never quite got off the ground to even building a gratitude journal community app before finally creating a media company focused on startups and entrepreneurs, I can't say I've taken the path of least resistance. It's been long, hard, and frustrating but also exciting, gratifying, and fun. I have new gray hairs (or they could be summer blondes) popping up daily that I now attribute to this journey. And along the way, I've taken lots of notes.

I've observed that there are thousands of people with ideas who want to create something but don't know where to start. At the same time, I've observed massive shifts in technology and business that have reduced the costs and other barriers to starting a new venture.

I've noticed that the media has a love affair with successful startup founders and has glamorized tech startups. I've also noticed that many of those who are jumping into the startup game have very high expectations and are ill equipped to handle the realities of the journey, which can have devastating consequences.

Although I'm still very much on the journey myself—and probably always will be—I've learned a lot from my own experiences and those of others. So my goal is to offer a step-by-step guide, filled with my own stories, lessons, and observations, as well as many insights shared with me by fellow startup founders, partners, and industry leaders I've met along the way. Whether you're just out of school and starting to code a feature you think could catch on or have been around the block and need some inspiration or additional knowledge to fuel your endeavor, this book will help you along your own entrepreneurial adventure. No one can do it alone—we all need help and advice. Consider this book part of your extended network, where you can reach in and find nuggets of information whenever you need.

Each chapter starts with essential lessons and advice, followed by a section on the harsh reality of starting up. I want you to be as prepared as possible for the challenges of the journey—and it's a huge challenge. So I'll share stories about those worst-case scenarios and what-can-go-wrong-will-go-wrong situations. I've experienced working all-nighters, taking red-eye flights, running out of money, vacation-skipping, bootstrapping, negotiating, hiring and firing employees, and succumbing to stress-induced illness. Although these are real startup life realities, they are seldom discussed.

On the bright side, each chapter also has a section on celebrating and enjoying the journey. We'll cover how to celebrate the startup life and all of your advantages and successes, big and small. I'm a firm believer that the incredible difficulty of starting up is all the more reason to stop, exhale, share, thank, and appreciate all the positive moments along the way.

The purpose of this book is to inspire and give you an overview of the journey you're embarking on. If you have questions along the way, we've designed an online companion at http://tech.co/book to help guide you and provide more resources and tools.

Maybe you'll be the next [insert today's most famous startup founder here] or maybe you'll turn your idea into a product or service that can become a solid business, earning you steady revenue. We all have different goals. My goal is to help you navigate and enjoy the startup journey, staying healthy and optimistic as you pursue your passion. So let's get started!

Part 1
Getting Started

1 Entrepreneurial Mind

Fortune favors the bold.

—Virgil

My 10-year journey from college to starting up taught me how to think like an entrepreneur and embrace the startup life, a life that I am firmly planted in and thankful for every day. My story may be different from yours, but you'll probably recognize some elements and be able to learn from my mistakes and my observations.

After growing up in the cornfields of northern Illinois dreaming of a baseball career, I realized in college that it wasn't meant to be, so I decided to jump into computer technology. My computer technology degree from Purdue University landed me a summer internship my junior year with a consulting company in what was then the Sears Tower in downtown Chicago. I was getting paid $20 an hour for the summer, which at the time was a lot for a college student who looked more like a 15-year-old.

The internship turned into a full-time opportunity and I took it. It wasn't the Chicago Cubs, but the Internet boom was still young and I was close to home and my favorite sports teams. I learned a number of things working at a fast-paced, scrappy technology consulting business. The first was that you don't have to actually have a product to sell it. We sold work that was not yet created off the idea that we could create it in just a short time. This was a new concept to me and one that has helped me sell our Tech Cocktail vision not based on where we've been but on where we're going.

It wasn't until the spring after September 11, 2001, that I learned the hardest lesson. The company wasn't doing as well as it previously had, and there was a cash-flow shortage, so they had to lay off nearly the entire team, including me and many of the colleagues I had helped hire. It was a sad day. I remember walking home in the cold Chicago rain. Getting laid off from my first job out of college taught me a very important lesson: *there is no security in working for someone else.* I had been raised believing that if you go out and work really hard, you can get a good job, build a career, and everything will fall into place. What they don't tell you is that some of the companies you work for may also need to make changes to survive, at your expense. You might not get a shot at building the career you imagined no matter how hard you work.

But I still wasn't a rebel yet, so I went to work for a larger corporation, the Tribune Company, with the sense that it would be *more* secure. It had been around almost a hundred years, and I had grown up visiting the iconic Tribune Tower across from the Wrigley Building on Michigan Avenue. It was a Chicago media icon. So when I landed a job with the Tribune, I was sure I had found the place I was going to build a career—not to mention, they owned the Chicago Cubs. This meant I could see more Cubs games than ever before. I loved working at the Tribune and walking into the tower every day. It was a dream come true for me. But even though Tribune Company adapted early to get newspapers online, I started to realize that they were not aggressive enough—startups like Yahoo! and AOL were land-grabbing for niche industry news eyeballs online, and companies such as Craigslist and Google devastated the online classified and display advertising space.

While still at Tribune, I started my own personal blog called *Somewhat Frank* to review startups and better understand blogging, and I started to see things that needed improvement in the fast-paced blogosphere. And I was a developer, so I was in an interesting position. I realized I could literally develop a product to solve a problem, launch it via my blog, and acquire new users instantly. So I did just that.

At the time, spam blogs, or splogs, were a problem. I noticed that popular entrepreneur, investor, and blogger Mark Cuban, also the owner of the Dallas Mavericks, had been posting in the blogosphere about it. He was hot on the topic of splogs because he had invested in a blog search engine called IceRocket, which was getting infiltrated by spam blogs. Sploggers were churning out thousands of landing pages filled with ads for popular search terms, polluting the Web.

When I realized this, I sprang into action. A friend of mine and I spent our nights after work creating a simple product called Splog Reporter, with the mission of helping clean up the blogosphere one splog at a time. The term *splog* hadn't existed more than a few days earlier, and we had already built a product to help tackle it. It took off! Within days, I started getting interviews and Splog Reporter was covered by the *Wall Street Journal, Wired,* and a number of other publications— even the *Toronto Star* picked up the story.

Splog Reporter lasted only about three months before we had to pull the plug. I realized that in order to really help IceRocket and other blog search engines clean up their indexes, while creating a sustainable business, I would have to build a comprehensive search engine, which was a bit out of scope for my first venture. It was a good decision, as Google then added their own blog search engine, crushing the competition, as it would have done to Splog Reporter.

Although short-lived, Splog Reporter had two pretty big impacts on me. First, I got to connect with Mark Cuban—that was a pretty memorable experience. Being mentioned in the same *Wall Street Journal* article as him was amazing. Second, Splog Reporter was my own little startup 101 course. It was a huge aha moment for me. I started to see problems as opportunities to build something. I now knew that with my coding abilities, I could launch a product, get users, and make lots of noise. I had a voice. What did I need my day job for, again? Oh, that's right: to make money to pay my mortgage, student loans, and car payment. But this was when I realized I could do it—I could startup.

All these experiences, and a few others I'll get to, rewired my brain from believing I needed someone else to give me a stable job to being excited about venturing out on my own. I learned that you don't have to follow the old ways and rules—rules that were making traditional companies struggle. I was finally ready to start Tech Cocktail, which is how I came to write this book and share my stories with all of you.

So what lessons can we learn from my story? Let's dive in and look at what it means to think like an entrepreneur and how to make sure you have the right mind-set to build a startup. Although not everyone is comfortable with the uncertainty or adventure that comes with entrepreneurship—or has the vision it takes to create something from nothing—it's possible to train your brain to be more alert to opportunities, question rules, and constantly be in learning mode. Just being aware of this mode of thinking should help you better understand your own thought patterns and slowly and gradually shift them to the creative but focused, risk-taking but prudent, optimistic but failure-embracing attitude of the entrepreneur.

See Problems as Opportunities

Thinking entrepreneurially starts with thinking a little differently. Most people get caught up with self-imposed barriers that blind them to what's possible. This type of thought might start out with, "I'd like to, but I can't because ... " Entrepreneurs don't allow their minds to be shut off by these types of "I'd like to but ... " statements. They understand there may be potential barriers, but they're able to look past them. They see barriers as adventures, as the beginning of something big, and as the means to make something amazing happen.

Vision

I've witnessed two types of entrepreneurs: those who love the process of entrepreneurship, no matter the product or service (they just love the challenge), and those with a strong background in a particular field who see a way to improve it. The former is a creator, someone who probably couldn't fathom the idea of working for someone else and may be a lifelong serial entrepreneur. The latter often has a stronger vision, as this person knows the field better than anyone else and sees something that no one else can.

Do you have a strong vision for a better world? The vision that has propelled Tech Cocktail is to help entrepreneurs gain visibility locally and nationally and enjoy their startup life journey. To do that, we provide them with connections, community, and resources (news, reports, events, and more).

Think Less; Act More

The idea of going out and getting started is encapsulated in slogans such as "Just do it," made popular by Nike. Sayings such as "Get shit done" or "Ready, fire, aim" (also the name of a book by Michael Masterson) have helped make these ideas more mainstream in the startup world. I always like to use "just start" as a battle cry for anyone sitting on the fence about the best time to unleash his or her idea into the world.

Saras Sarasvathy, an associate professor at the University of Virginia's Darden School of Business, has done extensive research into how entrepreneurs' brains work. She studied 27 entrepreneurs who had companies that had revenues ranging from $200 million to $6.5 billion and had started multiple companies with both successes and failures. She gave them case studies of problems faced by startups and asked them to talk through the problems while being recorded. And she found a major difference in the way entrepreneurs and nonentrepreneurs think.

What Sarasvathy observed is that entrepreneurs use effectual reasoning. Entrepreneurs assess the tools that they have, come up with goals on the fly, and keep adapting to new circumstances and new information. In other words, thinking and action happen at the same time. Nonentrepreneurs tend to prefer causal reasoning, kind of a cause-and-effect way of thinking, where they start off with a long-term goal and plot out the best means to achieve it. In essence, nonentrepreneurs think before they act. Although this continues to be the model many parents and educational settings thrust on young minds, entrepreneurs are less likely to follow it.

Always Learning

Remaining curious has helped me tremendously throughout the years. If I hadn't sat in on that important blogging session in New Orleans, explored the various blog platforms on my own, and learned about RSS and what it was doing to deliver content to people, it would have been harder for me to understand what this little but disruptive RSS-enabling startup named Feed-Burner was doing in Chicago. I never would have met Dick Costolo, Matt Shobe, Steve Olechowski, Rick Klau, Don Loeb, or my Tech Cocktail cofounder Eric Olson. I never would have been introduced to Jen Consalvo, who was at AOL building products that leveraged RSS and working with FeedBurner at the time. She would never have joined me to take on Tech Cocktail full-time. I didn't know where all these things would lead me. But I let curiosity and serendipity be my guide. Looking back everything looks so logical—like I planned it out that way—but I didn't.

In life and in business, I am a firm believer in lifelong learning and keeping an open mind. In business, you need to take in and learn as much as possible from customers, competitors, and even other industries. At the same time, you need to constantly add on new skills such as leadership, marketing, funding, accounting—everything in this book.

Dick Costolo

In 2003, Dick Costolo cofounded the RSS tool FeedBurner with Eric Lunt, Steve Olechowski, and Matt Shobe. FeedBurner was acquired by Google in 2007, and Costolo went on to spend time there working on ads. He left to become chief operating officer (COO) of Twitter in 2009 and replaced Evan Williams as chief executive officer (CEO) in 2010. Costolo is based in San Francisco.

Jen Consalvo

Jen Consalvo is the cofounder and COO of Tech Cocktail. She has worked in product development for more than a decade, leading large and small teams in a range of areas such as digital imaging, community and social platforms, syndication, and personalization. The majority of her career was at AOL, planning and building products used by millions of people globally. Jen also cofounded Shiny Heart Ventures, which developed Thankfulfor, a gratitude journaling community. Jen is an angel investor in the DC group NextGen Angels and author of *Love Your Photos: A Simple Guide to Photographic Happiness.*

Risk

To startup, you need to be at one with risk. That doesn't mean being a risk lover. I'm certainly not—but I do have a high tolerance for risk. You have to be okay with being tight on money, time, and resources.

There are a few things you can do to minimize risk. Being passionate about the idea actually lowers the risk, because you get more intrinsic value and happiness from working on it. For some people, the real risk is staying in a dead-end job and regretting it later in life. There will always be another great-paying, comfy, 9-to-5 desk job waiting for you if you ever want to quit the startup life.

On the business side, entrepreneurs actually minimize risk as much as possible by testing hypotheses and talking to customers. In fact, Sarasvathy identified something she calls the affordable loss principle: entrepreneurs choose courses of action where they can afford to fail, limiting risk. Like the poker player who leaves most of his bankroll at home, they don't bet the farm on any one uncertain decision.

Rule Breaker

I loved coloring books as a kid. However, I didn't like staying in the lines, preferring to add personal flair to the images and make them my own. In some ways, those were my early rule-breaker startup genes oozing out. Startup founders are rule breakers; they don't stay in the lines. Look at the commercials for iconic companies, such as Apple, which says, "Think different" and "Here's to the crazy ones." These are geared at people who reject rules and the status quo in an effort to change the world—people who won't be ignored.

Entrepreneurs often have trouble working a regular job, and don't want to take directions from bosses they disagree with. They're generally stubborn in the sense that they believe their ideas and creations are better than the current options. It takes a little bit of an ego to think this way.

Entrepreneurs reject the rules about what can and can't be done; they reject the corporate standards of marketing, public relations (PR), design, work hours, and dress codes. They prefer to be fun, funny, or original; they work whenever they want, wearing whatever they want.

Optimism

Optimism is another characteristic trait of entrepreneurs. According to a survey done by Deloitte in October 2013, 82 percent of entrepreneurs thought their business would grow by at least 10 percent in the following year. This is *some* optimism, given that so many businesses fail. Along those lines, research by Harvard Business School senior lecturer Shikhar Ghosh suggests that 75 percent of venture-funded startups don't return investors' money and 30 to 40 percent completely go out of business. With such high failure rates, entrepreneurs have to be optimistic.

Although entrepreneurs don't believe in predicting the future, their optimism tells them that they can create it. This stems from seeing failures as learning experiences: even if they have a failure, they can still keep going. They're unstoppable because there is always another option. LivingSocial cofounder (and CEO until January 2014) Tim O'Shaughnessy says, "Until you don't have any more money as a company, there's always a play ... One of the best characteristics of a CEO is [knowing] there's always a play—people may not see it, but you have the ability to."

How can you cultivate optimism? Michael Buckbee of Optimization Robot

LivingSocial

LivingSocial is a daily deals website that offers discounts to consumers based on a group buying model. The DC-based company grew out of a studio called Hungry Machine (launched in 2007), which built apps for Facebook. When they saw that deals could be a huge opportunity, they set aside their other efforts to focus solely on LivingSocial. Today, LivingSocial has raised hundreds of millions of dollars in funding and has more than 60 million members.

One suggests a trick from Conan O'Brien and improv comedy. He says to act as if what you're doing is completely normal: meeting big-name investors, huge corporate partners, or high-profile journalists. Just tell yourself it's normal, like it's a comedy act. Pretend the obstacles aren't a big deal—mind over matter.

Whenever my COO starts to worry or get consumed by the challenges ahead, she stops and writes down as many positives about the company she can think of. She says it stops the fear in its tracks. You need this optimistic outlook to make it through the ups and downs of the startup journey.

The Harsh Reality

Even if you think like an entrepreneur, it doesn't mean you're not afraid. Fear can be a great motivator. Chris Sonjeow, cofounder and chief marketing officer (CMO) at LoveBook, calls entrepreneurs confident worriers. NewFoundry CEO Richard Chang says, "Does it scare you? Good. If you aren't afraid, then it isn't challenging enough."

Sarah Evans takes this attitude. A PR and social media expert, she decided to create a life mission statement: "I run unabashedly free through this one life without fear. I believe in the unexpected, I believe in abundance." But that doesn't mean she doesn't fear anything. Instead, she uses fear as a compass—telling her to head in that direction, because it will make her a better person. "Fear is also something that can motivate me. As soon as I feel afraid about something, I know

Sarah Evans

Sarah Evans is a "social media freak," consulting on social media and media training through her company, Sevans Strategy. She was the creator of #journchat, a weekly, live Twitter chat for public relations professionals, journalists, and bloggers. Evans runs and writes for *FAVES + CO.*, a blog about social and tech news, and is the author of the book *[RE]FRAME: Little Inspirations for a Larger Purpose.* She also spent a year as chief evangelist at Las Vegas startup Tracky.

that I have to do it," she says, whether that's move across the country to Vegas, do public speaking, or take on more responsibility.

Dina Kaplan, a cofounder of Blip, struggled with crippling fears early on but didn't realize it. Overwhelmed and overloaded by work, she was afraid to hire employees because she feared she didn't deserve them and would be a bad manager. Kaplan never invited her entrepreneur friends to hang out, because she feared they didn't really like her. When Facebook COO Sheryl Sandberg e-mailed her asking to meet up, Kaplan didn't reply because she worried about wasting Sandberg's time. This all led to panic attacks, and Kaplan becoming afraid of simply walking down the street.

> ### Dina Kaplan
>
> With a background in TV reporting and production, Dina Kaplan cofounded Blip in 2005. As it grew, Blip transformed from a video platform and distributor to a video destination, showcasing the best Web series. Based in New York and Los Angeles, Blip now attracts more than 30 million viewers per month. It was acquired by Maker Studios in 2013. When we last heard from Kaplan, she had gone on a life-changing trip around the world and was contemplating her next move.

But like a true entrepreneur, she learned to conquer her fears. She took time off to travel and forced herself to go scuba diving, zip-lining, and bungee jumping, all activities she was deathly afraid of. And it changed her life. Now, she asks for what she wants. Instead of saying what people want to hear, she is authentic and honest—even with venture capitalists. Every day, Kaplan now asks herself: "What would my life look like if I lived without fear? What would I do if I lived without fear?"

In school we are generally taught to be causal thinkers, in Sarasvathy's words. An MBA program teaches you to have a predetermined goal and figure out the best means to achieve it—for example, deciding on a target market for an advertising campaign. We grow up learning to think like good employees, which includes following the vision of others, following rules set by others, repeating the same tasks over and over, and doing more planning to avoid risks.

It's hard to rewire our brains and change the way we think. It took me a decade, so don't be hard on yourself if you don't jump off the entrepreneurial diving board upon reading this book. It might take some time to get your wires reset.

Celebrate: Enjoy the Journey

As an entrepreneur, I am grateful for every day I have the freedom to create and share ideas that could have a positive effect on the world. I think gratitude is an important part of being a happy entrepreneur. A few years ago, I felt so strongly about it that I developed a gratitude community and application called Thankfulfor (http://thankfulfor.com) with Jen Consalvo, my partner and the COO of Tech Cocktail. The idea was to create a simple place to capture and share your gratitude—and in doing so, celebrate the things you have. It's a passion-fueled side project that helps remind us that no one can do anything alone.

Entrepreneur Gary Vaynerchuk—CEO of VaynerMedia and author of *The Thank You Economy*—knows that better than anyone. His life is infused with gratitude for his parents, who brought him from the former Soviet Union to the United States. And his attitude is an inspiration to any of us who forget to be grateful. "People have this entitlement thing—what are

Gary Vaynerchuk

Born in Belarus, Gary Vaynerchuk grew up in Edison, New Jersey, and eventually started helping out with his father's liquor store. That led to his creation of WineLibrary.com and the popular video series *Wine Library TV*. In 2009, Vaynerchuk and his brother AJ founded the social media agency VaynerMedia. The company has since grown to a team of more than 250 and worked with brands such as GE, Pepsi, and the New York Jets. Based in New York City, Vaynerchuk is an angel investor in startups such as Tumblr, Path, and Uber, and he's the author of *Crush It!*, *The Thank You Economy*, and (most recently) *Jab, Jab, Jab, Right Hook*.

you going to do for me and then I'll give you something. I hate that!" he says. "Being an immigrant, you're not entitled. I didn't expect anything. We had to claw and scrap for everything, and that's how I roll now. And even as I've become a bigger presence in this space … I'm still so grateful."

The principles of gratitude can apply to your everyday life as well as your entrepreneurial life. One of the ways to enjoy the startup life—despite the roller coaster of challenges and stress—is to remain grateful for its enormous benefits. For example, you don't have to deal with a bad boss or worry about losing your vacation days. You are in charge of your destiny; you get to experience that feeling of ownership, pride, and potential for growth and huge success.

Bo Fishback, the CEO of Zaarly, says, "I can't even imagine working in a big, slow company right now. Whenever I get too stressed out, I think, 'What else on earth would I rather be doing?'"

Final Thoughts

Whether you're creating a teleportation device, building an app, or running a new media company—no matter how small or big your project—realize that you're changing the world.

"You become a true architect of life. You get to create ideas, create jobs, find better ways of doing things, so it's really an enjoyable experience," says Uassist.ME founder Alfredo Atanacio. And I couldn't agree with him more.

2 Ideas

Ideas are like rabbits. You get a couple and learn how to handle them, and pretty soon you have a dozen.

—John Steinbeck

W e've all been there—something happens, we lose the keys, burn the eggs, or kill the car battery. If only there was a way we could prevent or quickly remedy the problem. Brainstorming begins—boom!—and an idea is born from necessity.

Are you a person who's just flowing with ideas? Or do you have trouble coming up with them? The easiest way to find an idea may be to follow your obsessions—that's what MakerBot chief executive officer (CEO) Bre Pettis did.

Pettis was a teacher and a maker. He grew up fixing things, then taught art in public schools. He eventually found himself working at *Maker* magazine, where he had to deliver a video every Friday showing how he made something, such as hovercrafts, lasers, and other cool gadgets. After some time at Etsy—a marketplace for makers—he started a side project, called MakerBot, that leveraged his knowledge for making things. MakerBot grew organically and eventually took over Pettis's life. It caught on with a group of makers just as obsessed as Pettis.

But it wasn't easy. At one point, Pettis sold everything he owned to buy more robot parts to keep the company going. He remembers thinking, "I'm not letting this thing go until it eats me." Thankfully, it did not eat him alive—but it did take him on a startup journey to the forefront of a budding industry, 3D printing. And MakerBot was positioned to enable consumers to use 3D printing to change the world and make it a better place. Its users did just that.

In 2013, Richard Van As and Ivan Owen created a design for a Robohand, a set of 3D printed fingers that can open and close based on wrist motions. Printed on a MakerBot, Robohand can replace custom-made versions (which can cost $10,000 per finger) for around $150. Liam, a five-year-old in South Africa with a congenital disorder affecting his fingers, got one of the first Robohands. As he outgrows it, he'll be able to get another—as will others who couldn't afford a traditional prosthetic. This is just one example of why Pettis and MakerBot are obsessed with what they do.

This chapter covers how to find the idea that's right for you and common questions you might have along the way.

Scratch Your Own Itch

Pettis's idea evolved from a passion, but sometimes the best ideas come from problems that you want to solve for yourself. Take 37signals, a Chicago-based design and development firm that needed a way to communicate with clients. The existing options were too clunky and bloated, so they decided to build their own and called it Basecamp. Now used by millions of people, Basecamp was born when 37signals (now called Basecamp) scratched their own itch: they found a problem they had and built a product that others could use as well.

Banjo, a social discovery app, was born out of Damien Patton's missed connection. Fifteen years after serving in Desert Storm, he found himself in the same airport as one of his fellow servicemen, who lived across the country. He hadn't seen his friend for all those years, and they didn't see each other that day either—none of their social networks could alert them. So Patton set out to create an app that would feed you relevant information, such as friends nearby, without you having to ask.

But how do you come up with an idea?

Throughout your regular day, you may encounter a problem or something inefficient or irritating. Carry a notepad or use your mobile device, and write it down. No need to come up with a solution or product right now; just look at the world with a problem-oriented eye. Jay Alan Samit, president of ooVoo, tells his students to write down five things that bother them or could be improved each day, creating a list of dozens of ideas in a month. You'll have a lot to work with and should be able to find a problem you're obsessed with.

While writing for my personal blog and guest blogging for TechCrunch, I took several trips to Silicon Valley, where I met numerous startup founders, entrepreneurs, investors, and pundits. I noticed that many of these folks saw each other regularly at San Francisco events, *like every week,* where they met, chatted, and shared information. I took note and brought nuggets back to the Windy City to see if there were similar opportunities.

When I did not see any events that had the same San Fran upstart vibe, I began to toy with the idea of starting something to help facilitate these interactions. I had seen what new media such as blogging could do and understood the importance of real-life events to bring together a community, so I began to noodle on an idea. After asking a few entrepreneurs what they thought, I started to reserve domain names for what this new venture might be called. I secured names like Techstir.com, TechBlendr.com, TechKoolaid.com, TechMixr.com, and TechCocktail.com. I had found an idea; now I wanted to find a cofounder.

Go After an Industry

If you haven't found a problem out in the wild, look closer to home. If you're familiar with an industry, you already have contacts and personal connections who could give you an advantage. You speak the language, and you know how it works. You're also familiar with major players and competition, big obstacles such as regulations, and more. This industry expertise will help you see things that others cannot.

Here's an example: Dan Stratman was a pilot and worked in the airline industry for 23 years before starting Airport Life, an airport application that includes flight statuses, airport restaurants, and baggage policies. It would be hard for an outsider to figure out how to pull in all that real-time information, but he knew where to look for it, which gave him an advantage.

As for me, I worked for the Tribune and AOL, both giant media companies, for years. I was one of the early contributors to TechCrunch, along with my personal blog *Somewhat Frank*. I had industry experience in new media platforms and connections with startups to get me started.

You have industry knowledge as well; you just need to determine what it is. To research, go out for coffee or breakfast with people in your chosen industry. Ask them about problems they have or areas that need fixing. The idea is to always be looking for ways these people or organizations might become customers.

Debate: Should You Build Painkillers or Vitamins?

No, you're not jumping into the pharmaceutical industry, but the common advice for entrepreneurs is to build painkillers rather than vitamins. Don Dodge, an investor, startup veteran, and developer advocate at Google, calls painkillers a must-have. They could be something that increases return on investment (ROI), improves sales, or helps companies satisfy a regulatory requirement—it's really *needed*. On the other hand, a vitamin is something that's nice to have. Productivity tools, collaboration platforms, analytical tools—any kind of tools—tend to be vitamins.

> **Don Dodge**
>
> Don Dodge is a developer advocate at Google, where he helps independent developers work with Google platforms. He came to Google from Microsoft, where he was a startup evangelist. Before that, Dodge worked at pioneering startups such as Forte Software, AltaVista, Napster, Bowstreet, and Groove Networks. He is also an angel investor.

With a painkiller idea, people are more likely to pay for it and remain loyal customers. They're also more likely to find you even if you don't have a huge marketing budget. You're solving a real problem, and these people are probably already out there searching for a solution.

These painkillers are known to soar higher, but some vitamins do very well. Products such as Facebook, Instagram, and Pinterest were

not created to solve an obvious user problem, but they have had staying power and generated huge demand. Sarah Tavel, a senior associate
at Bessemer Venture Partners, calls this category a drug; it's something
that's nice to have that becomes addictive and hard to give up. Ever-
note, for example, uses a freemium pricing model to give people a taste
(for free) and get them hooked so they'll upgrade to a premium plan.
A number of other companies use the same model.

Remember, different products appeal to different people—
something that's a vitamin to one group may be a drug or a painkiller
to another. For example, a meditation app might be a painkiller for
someone who gets panic attacks but a vitamin for a mildly stressed
parent. Keep the painkiller/vitamin/drug distinction in mind when
coming up with and sorting through your ideas and target market.

But don't give up if you don't get the support you expected. Matt
Mullenweg, creator of WordPress, didn't, even when the world told
him they didn't need another blogging platform. "Some of the most
interesting things come from doing what everyone says is a bad idea or
where no one else is interested—those ideas that you almost have to
ram down the world's throat. Even if you fail, at least you weren't failing
at the same thing everyone else was doing," he says. The founders of
GrubHub followed this advice, persisting in their dream of online
food ordering even when everyone in 2004 thought that the idea of
ordering food from your computer was crazy. Little did we know
everyone would be carrying a computer in their pocket as a mobile
and app revolution kicked into gear. And GrubHub certainly didn't
fail: merged with its largest competitor Seamless, the company now
has more than 600 employees, processes about 150,000 orders a day,
and helps people in more than 600 cities order food from more than
26,000 restaurants.

For a list of tools for coming up with ideas, check out http://tech
.co/book.

The Harsh Reality

Coming up with ideas takes time. It's difficult to come up with ideas when you sit down and try to think of them. The best ideas come to you naturally or organically. Keep notes in your everyday flow, and you should be able to capture some good ones.

You may come up with a genius idea only to discover that it's been done before—no worries; a little competition never hurt anybody. Google launched when there were plenty of other search engines out there; Gmail came after Hotmail, AOL Mail, and Yahoo! Mail. The iPhone was not the first smartphone to launch, but it innovated on a trend. Some entrepreneurs see competition as validation for their idea. As much as you like the idea of being a visionary, you may consider working on someone else's idea and become their cofounder. It's even possible to buy ideas on various websites.

It's easy to fall in love with your idea, but be wary of getting too attached. You'll probably have to change it or pivot to survive and keep up with the environment around you—like these companies did:

- Twitter grew out of Odeo, a personal podcasting service.
- Instagram (bought by Facebook for $1 billion) was originally a location-based service called Burbn.
- Pinterest came from Tote, a shopping app that sent updates when items you liked went on sale.
- Flickr grew out of a game called Game Neverending.
- Groupon was originally The Point, a site for organizing around causes.
- LivingSocial started out as Hungry Machine, a small team making Facebook applications.
- Fab.com was originally a social network for gay men.

Groupon

Groupon grew out of The Point, a site for organizing around causes. The Point was struggling to get traction, but the team noticed an interesting campaign: people organizing around the "cause" of saving money, hoping to negotiate a discount if they all bought the same product. Groupon the daily deals website launched in Chicago in 2008, starting with restaurants and then expanding into products, getaways, live events, and luxury experiences. Groupon's initial public offering (IPO) took place in November 2011, and the company now has hundreds of millions of subscribers. It was cofounded by Andrew Mason, who was CEO until he was fired in February 2013.

Finally, your ideas aren't considered valuable—they are a commodity. Coming up with ideas is hard, but it's not the hardest part by any means. It's just the beginning of what will be a long, up-and-down startup journey.

Should you tell other people about your ideas? This is a huge debate that entrepreneurs have all the time. But someone has probably had the idea before, and execution is arguably more important than the idea. Not to mention that you may end up pivoting or changing your idea at some point. For these reasons, it's common practice for entrepreneurs to talk to venture capitalists or apply to accelerators without having them sign a nondisclosure agreement (NDA). Investors are not going to go out and copy your idea. What I'd be more worried about is an investor sharing your idea with a competitive startup in their portfolio, which has been known to happen. But the odds are pretty slim. As for sharing your idea with other entrepreneurs, most people won't have time to drop everything and work on your idea—they have their own to worry about.

Celebrate: Enjoy the Journey

Coming up with ideas is fun. I love it. Who doesn't love thinking big and trying to change the world? So enjoy the process and the eureka moment when you come up with a good one. Try to relish the idea generation stage, because you get to be so creative and think about problems worth solving. Entrepreneurs love this part of the process.

Chuck DeMonte of GrooveFox says it's "one of the best parts of being an entrepreneur, creating!"

"Coming up with new ideas is the best part of entrepreneurism!" echoes Jamie Walker, founder and CEO of SweatGuru. And idea generation doesn't stop once you have an idea to work on; you'll constantly be coming up with new ways to change it and tweak it to delight customers even more, evolve with a changing landscape, or expand your business.

One way to make sure you enjoy your startup journey is to ask yourself a few questions right from the beginning:

- Who do you want your customers to be?
- Do you want to sell directly to consumers or to businesses?
- Which type of consumers do you want to sell to—moms, male twentysomethings, rich people, poor people, fashionistas?
- Which type of businesses do you want to sell to—small businesses or big corporations?

Your customers are the people you'll be interacting with day in and day out, and you want to be sure you enjoy being around them. I love the passion and drive of entrepreneurs, and with Tech Cocktail I get to hang around, write about, and interact with them every day while also working with amazing brands that are interested in connecting with our audience online and off. So make sure you are comfortable with your chosen clients or customers.

Another question you should think about is this: How big of a problem do you want to solve? Do you have a passion to change the world? Or change your community? Or an industry?

If you're more interested in money, this aspect is less important. But if passion is something you're looking for, you'll have more fun along the startup journey if you pick a project that's meaningful to you. You'll also have a greater chance of making it through the tough times.

Final Thoughts

Ask yourself if your idea is something you're willing to be obsessed about for the next 5 or 10 years. If not, there may be another idea that you would love to do for the long haul. Be patient; it will come to you.

Bre Pettis is a shining example of following your passion. When MakerBot released its first 20 prototypes, thinking they'd take two months to sell, they sold out instantly.

"I didn't realize how important [being obsessive] was," says Pettis. "We were just obsessed with getting it the best it could possibly be with the resources we had at hand. That meant that I answered all the support e-mails and support calls for the first two and a half years—and then it turns out that's not normal, other people just hire people at that point," he laughs. "If you're not obsessed with your product, f*** it, screw it, or don't do it! . . . Kill it right now and get on to the next thing."

Today, there are more than 35,000 MakerBot machines in the wild. The company raised $10 million in funding and was then acquired by Stratasys for $403 million in June 2013. And it all started with a maker, a teacher, and his obsession.

3 Action

The way to get started is to quit talking and begin doing.

—Walt Disney

I've launched many products over the past 15 years, some being my own initiatives, others for the companies I've worked with. Through it all, the part that gets me most excited is the beginning—those first steps where you have no limitations. You've got your idea, and now it's time to dive in! You get to start dreaming about the future, filling in the details, and laying the foundation for what can be a fulfilling, creative, wild ride.

When ideas are new, the sky's the limit, which can also be overwhelming and stop people in their tracks. As I've traveled from city to city across the United States, I've talked to thousands of people who have ideas. Some people have started working on them; others haven't. I've often wondered what separates the two.

Jessica Kim is one of the starters I met. She refused to let inexperience hold her back with BabbaCo, a lifestyle brand that she hoped would become the "Martha Stewart of baby." She started out with an idea for a simple cover for a baby's car seat called the BabbaCover, but immediately realized she did not know how to sew to build a prototype!

For a lot of people, this dream would have been dead. But not for Kim. She taught herself to sew by watching YouTube videos—and in a pinch, glue and staples came in handy to finish areas where she ran into sewing problems. *In short, she hacked it.*

With a prototype in hand, she pulled in a partner she knew well from her previous venture. Together they were able to commercialize the product, getting it into a thousand locations within a year. They also got accepted into a Chicago-based startup accelerator currently run by Troy Henikoff called Excelerate Labs (now rebranded as Techstars Chicago), which provided mentorship, advice, and encouragement as they turned this single-product company into a monthly subscription service for children's activities.

You can become a starter as well. To help, here are some of the things I've done when I've come up with a new idea:

- *Whiteboard it or do a brain dump.* Start by writing it all out, sketching it, getting it out of your head, and giving it life.
- *Start talking* to trusted friends and family about it. Ideas locked in your mind have no room to expand.
- *Give it a name.* Even though it may be premature, even coming up with a code name for the project will give it momentum.
- *Do research around it.* Look for anything that comes close to being a competitor. Finding competitors is a good thing because it helps validate that your idea has a market and give you ideas for differentiation!

While you're taking these first steps, you'll also want to start thinking about a few important questions.

Who Are Your Customers?

Chapter 5 will focus in-depth on the importance and how-tos of customer development and finding product-market fit, the fundamental building block of any company. As a new mom, Kim knew her customers well—and that's what helped her engage them and create community.

What Would a Simple Prototype Look Like?

You can think big, but it's good to start small. In the product-market fit chapter, we'll get more into how to start lean, test your concept, and keep steering in the right direction. Kim's first BabbaCover was hand-sewn and not the most professional-looking product in the world—but people still wanted it.

How Much Personal Investment Do You Want to Make?

A startup business is a risky investment, so another way to phrase this question is: How much can you afford to lose? Your initial costs might include things such as hosting, acquisition of domain names, design, legal, and marketing. Over time, these costs will only grow.

If you're married or financially connected with someone else, consult with that person before you start investing in the company to avoid uncomfortable discussions later and the possibility of sleeping on the couch. Cash flow keeps the business afloat, so as a startup founder you have to manage your expenses. If you're daring enough, you could do as some entrepreneurs have done and go live in a country with a low cost of living (for example, somewhere in Southeast Asia or Central America) while building your initial product. Domestically, look at places such as downtown Las Vegas, Detroit, Kansas City, Des Moines, San Antonio, St. Louis, or Indianapolis as other low-cost living options. Or downsize or move in with parents or friends. We've seen many entrepreneurs make large and small life changes to pursue their ideas.

Do You Want to Quit Your Job?

Do you have a full-time job and plan to work nights and weekends on your idea? Can you work a part-time job? Or are you going all-in from the beginning as a full-time entrepreneur? Only you can decide which approach is the one for you.

There is an ongoing debate on whether you can succeed while you still have a full-time job. They can take up valuable mind space, so even if you have enough time for your startup, you may not have enough mental and emotional capacity.

On the plus side, a full-time job gives you income, so there's less risk. Putting pressure on your startup to start paying the bills immediately is distracting and may cause you to make the wrong decisions, focusing on short-term money and not on long-term success or satisfaction.

Tech Cocktail started as a passion project. Both myself and my cofounder were working full-time and kept Tech Cocktail going in our free time. Luckily, my employer, AOL, realized the value of Tech Cocktail as a way to keep an ear to the rail on the latest early-stage startups and the tech startup community. Every employer is different.

There have been many successful companies that started as side projects. BabyList, a baby registry, was built as a side project when Natalie Gordon was pregnant with her son. They got into the 500 Startups accelerator in 2012, raised $620,000, and saw 10,000 registries created in the first half of 2013. The global marketplace Craigslist grew from group e-mails that Craig Newmark was sending to his friends about San Francisco events. Eventually he quit his job but still freelanced while continuing to build Craigslist on the side. Today, Craigslist hovers around the eleventh most popular site in the United States (according to Alexa), attracting millions of monthly visitors.

Another example is LivingSocial, which started out as Hungry Machine, a hybrid consultancy/startup with four cofounders: Tim O'Shaughnessy, Aaron Batalion, Eddie Frederick, and Val Aleksenko. At any given time, to pay the bills, at least two of them were working on consulting gigs and one was working on a Hungry Machine app. When a consulting job ended, they rotated so no one got bored. "Life didn't suck entirely; it just sucked most of the time," Batalion jokes. They built lots of apps, including Visual Bookshelf and something called Pick Your 5, where you could list five things you cared about. But when it became clear that the daily deals opportunity could be huge, they set aside their other projects and went all in.

If you decide to burn the midnight oil, too, here are some tips that might help you.

- *Check your employment contract* to make sure you're allowed to work on side projects, because it could legally belong to your employer.
- *Plan.* If you plan well, you'll always know what the next task on your to-do list is so you can dive in if you have a free half hour.

- *Set expectations with friends and family* so they know you're busy even after work hours while you're embarking on your startup journey.

- *Don't use company resources* on your startup. The last thing you want is to create an amazing business and have your company come after you because you were using their printer or computer. It's not worth the stress or time.

And here are the last two questions to keep in mind:

What Would Your Dream Team Look Like?

Put yourself in the future—imagine you've built something with legs that has taken off and you now have the resources to build your dream team. Who would be on it? Do you know people you would love to eventually hire? Even if it's years away, it's helpful to keep a list of rock-stars who might someday be part of your team. Future chapters will look at team building and company culture, which starts at the very beginning.

Who Else Can Help You?

Whether this is your first startup or not, it's wise to find mentors and advisors who can help you. Mentors can act as sounding boards, help you through issues they've experienced before, and connect you to their industry contacts. Start thinking about the people you look up to who could give you guidance. Chapter 11 talks more about the importance of building relationships.

Starting Simple

After I had the initial idea for Tech Cocktail, I was in search of a cofounder. One of the last things I had done at Tribune was work with a company called FeedBurner, a hot startup at the time led by Dick Costolo, now the chief executive officer (CEO) of Twitter. Through my contact on the publisher development team, Rick Klau, I was introduced to one of FeedBurner's new hires, a guy named Eric Olson. Klau thought we might get along, as Eric and his girlfriend had just left Boston to move into a sight-unseen Chicago apartment from Craigslist, to work at a startup. I knew I had to meet this guy. Aside from a mutual interest in startups, Eric was also a baseball fan. He loved the Boston Red Sox, and we commiserated about the Red Sox and Cubs' long pennant-less drought. Needless to say, we hit it off. Finding a cofounder is kind of like dating, and this first date was off the charts.

Eric had seen the growing Boston tech startup community and participated in local events up and down the East Coast. So when he got to Chicago, he was in search of similar opportunities to connect with the community and was considering starting something himself. It seemed like a great match. I decided to share my ideas with him about starting a company of some kind to better connect and amplify the local tech startup scene in Chicago, and Eric—working for one of the hottest startups in the city—was excited. We decided to team up and fill the void together.

We started by hosting an event that showcased local tech startups and invited the rest of the Chicago tech community to join us. But we needed a name. I'd registered a number of domains a few weeks earlier and shared them with Eric. Tech Cocktail didn't resonate at first, but as you can see from the e-mail that follows, it started to grow on us.

Hey Frank,

The logos look great. I like the second one best (just the oversized martini glass rather than the person w/ the glass). Its super simple and gets the point across. I like the name Tech Cocktail more and more. The cocktail part not only represents that fact that drinks are involved but it also represents the mix of people in the room (VCs, techies, entrepreneurs, etc.). I think this could be big.:-)

—Eric

The rest is history. We set a date of July 6, 2006, picked a venue, and, through e-mail and word of mouth, invited the community. At this first event, we showcased six early-stage tech startup companies and attracted close to 250 attendees. People from larger corporations attended, along with press, investors, developers, designers, entrepreneurs, hackers, and creatives. The energy that day was amazing. Attendees were truly excited to meet up and see that there were others like themselves bringing new products to life in the city.

But first steps are first steps. The first Tech Cocktail event didn't make any money. It was pulled together with $500 from a local hosting company and donated wine from artist Hugh MacLeod of Gaping Void fame. The venue we had selected was so new, it didn't even have its liquor license yet, so we had to rely on an army of family and friends to help make sure everyone's glasses were full. We quickly learned a lot about hosting events, and eventually were able to figure out the offline and online business of Tech Cocktail, which relied on sponsors, advertisers, and ticket sales like most media companies do.

During this early startup period, my connections with Eric and FeedBurner led me to an amazing new opportunity in Washington, DC. In September 2006, I moved from my beloved Chicago to take on product development for the masses at the original Internet juggernaut, AOL. This opened up the door for Tech Cocktail events and coverage in DC, which we tackled with the help of DC native Nick O'Neill, who later went on to start the popular *AllFacebook* blog. Our first DC event was made even more memorable by a certain New Yorker in the wine business who reached out to support the event with free wine and sponsorship dollars. His e-mail follows:

I would love to be involved as a sponsor of the DC Cocktail.

I can offer FREE wine and would love to promo my WINE LIBRARY TV gig.:)

Let me know of any details and if we can make this happen, and if we could do anything else or you have any other needs, but I think this can be really cool!

Frank, I really think you and Eric are doing great stuff and WLTV would love to be doing some cool shizz with u guys!

Gary Vaynerchuk

Winelibrary.com

Director of Operations

Gary Vaynerchuk, then of Wine Library TV, is now a *New York Times* best-selling author, investor, and cofounder of VaynerMedia, a digital agency. Tech Cocktail in Washington, DC, in the spring of 2007, was the first tech event he ever attended along with his brother AJ.

To stay true to Eric's roots, next came Boston. Then, a new accelerator called Techstars in Boulder reached out to see how we could work together, so we visited Brad Feld and David Cohen to host an event around their first batch of startups. Eric and I were hosting quarterly events in Chicago and traveling to each city to make events happen. We started blogging about the startups that participated, attracting even more attention. Other cities saw what we were doing and reached out, inviting us to bring Tech Cocktail to their area. For more than three years we both continued working full-time jobs while working nights and weekends to keep Tech Cocktail going as a passion side project. But as social media channels grew, the events grew—at one point the Chicago event grew to 1,000 people! It was too much.

In late 2009, the day came where Eric and I had to decide whether to take Tech

Brad Feld

Brad Feld has been an investor and entrepreneur since the late 1980s. A leader in the Boulder startup scene, he cofounded the Techstars accelerator in 2006. Since then, Techstars has expanded to seven cities and has partnered with companies such as Nike, Sprint, and Kaplan to power its accelerators. As of this writing, the core Techstars programs have funded nearly 300 companies, of which 90 percent are either active or acquired.

Feld also cofounded and is now managing director of the venture capitalist firm Foundry Group. To share his knowledge, he is heading up a series of books called *Startup Revolution*, including *Startup Communities*, *Startup Life* (with his wife, Amy Batchelor), and *Startup Boards* (with Mahendra Ramsinghani).

David Cohen

David Cohen is the cofounder, managing partner, and CEO of Techstars. He got his experience as a serial entrepreneur, selling his companies Pinpoint Technologies and earFeeder.com. Today, he's an advisor and board member, works with the University of Colorado's entrepreneurship programs, and runs the Colorado chapter of the Open Angel Forum. He's the coauthor of *Do More Faster* (with Brad Feld).

Cocktail on full-time or move on. With AOL spinning out of Time Warner into its own company again, I had an opportunity to volunteer for a separation package, which I took. But it was not clear I would be able to safely jump into Tech Cocktail full-time and keep it afloat. I was leaving behind a six-figure salary, benefits, and the comfort of working for a large company. So I did like any reasonable human would do when placed squarely on the end of a diving board: I curled my toes on the edge, didn't look down, and jumped. It was a scary feeling to free fall for a while, but after a few months, I adjusted to full-time self-employment and found the business.

Eric had a different vision for his future and bigger opportunities on the immediate horizon. Thankfully, he saw my excitement for continuing to push Tech Cocktail ahead full-time with the goal of turning it into a world-class news and events company and agreed to let me go after it. Knowing the workload was too much to take on alone, I pulled a new partner into Tech Cocktail, Jen Consalvo, who had spent over a decade building community products for millions and managing teams at AOL. Together we relaunched the site, found more partners, advertisers and sponsors, added team members, tested new parts of the business, and bootstrapped our growth for another three years. It wasn't nearly as easy to do as we thought it would be, and there were many moments of uncertainty and sleepless nights, but we were both passionate about the vision and committed to enjoying the journey.

How Do You Find a Cofounder?

The ideal cofounder shares your values and is trustworthy. You need to be able to speak your mind without having to sugarcoat it, and know that your cofounder won't betray your confidence. A cofounder needs to have passion for your idea and the drive to tackle it. The last thing you want is someone who doesn't truly believe in what you're striving for. As you search, look for someone who has complementary skills and is open to dealing with conflict and disagreements.

Timothy Chi of WeddingWire advises you to find people who have a similar tolerance for risk and work well with you. Chi started three companies and has found three cofounders: one was his former colleague at Blackboard, the other was a peer of his wife's from business school, and the third was referred by a friend.

"The questions of risk profile and whether you will work well together are the toughest to assess," says Chi. "These are the types of issues that can cause significant risk to the business. That's why, to whatever extent possible, I recommend getting to know your potential cofounders early. Meet for lunches and dinners, and work on small projects together. Do whatever it is you need to take a 'test-drive' before you all commit to quitting your full-time jobs."

So how do you find cofounders? First, look at your friends and contacts. If no one comes to mind, then expand your search and ask around. Use your network of friends, family, and colleagues to do this. Get out there and pound the pavement by attending different events. Our Tech Cocktail events, Startup Weekend, and local tech- and developer-focused meetups could be great places to meet potential cofounders. There are also organizations such as FounderDating and CoFounders-Lab created for exactly this purpose.

Startup Weekend

Startup Weekend hosts 54-hour weekend events where people interested in entrepreneurship come together, form teams around ideas, and launch them. On Sunday night, the teams present to an audience and winners are crowned. Startup Weekend has more than 45,000 alumni and has hosted events in more than 400 cities and 110 countries. The company is based in Seattle.

It's important to not let the lack of a cofounder be an excuse for not starting up. If you start and do well, cofounders will find you; lots of great companies started this way. Automattic was founded in

January 2003 when Matt Mullenweg wrote a blog post about starting a new project (which would become WordPress, the online publishing platform). Mike Little offered to contribute and eventually became cofounder. By showing that he was serious about the idea, Mullenweg attracted a cofounder and other volunteers around him.

The Harsh Reality

Starting up is hard and intimidating. A lot of people have ideas they want to work on *someday*, but someday never comes; they don't know where to start, so they never do.

Through the years, I've met too many people who are waiting for the stars to align. *Today is the best day to start.* Not tomorrow, when you have more time—today.

But finding a cofounder takes time. Entrepreneur Gerome Sapp is a former NFL athlete and had trouble getting people to take his idea for Fluencr seriously. But he didn't give up; he ended up traveling all around the United States, attending Ruby on Rails meetups, and learning to code in case he had to build the app himself. In the end, he found two technical cofounders in Austin after searching for about four months.

One of my startup attempts was called CampusJabber, a social network for college campuses that had social commerce built in for selling books, stereo equipment, furniture, or whatever. I shared the idea with a colleague who quickly joined as a cofounder in a more silent capacity, with the promise to support it along financially if it showed signs of growth.

I was in the process of completing my master's degree in computer science from Northwestern University and thought its campus might make for a good testing ground. So I also shared the idea with an undergraduate friend who found it interesting. I envisioned him helping to market it on campus while I developed it online. I pulled him in, along with his roommate, who also showed interest in helping with the endeavor. Now half of the team was actually part of the demographic the offering was geared toward.

At the time, Facebook didn't really exist except on some limited, elite college campuses. MySpace was still being used as well, but it was like a carnival to your senses. It seemed like we all agreed there was an opportunity to create a social network that connected and shared updates on campus and also enabled social commerce.

I later learned that we did *not* all agree on the vision. Because of their heavy involvement in student government on campus, the two undergrads felt that CampusJabber should focus heavily on student government. I did not. And aside from the initial vision, we didn't divide the labor equally. I was doing all the research, coding, writing, business development, and marketing while the rest of the team gave me feedback and went to class.

Needless to say, CampusJabber wasn't able to go anywhere, and after just a few months, I shut the site down. There were no hard feelings between the cofounders, but I learned that I would have been better off hiring them all as consultants or just asking them for advice rather than making them part of the business. So I cannot emphasize enough the importance of clearly communicating your vision with potential cofounders to ensure that you see eye to eye. If you don't, you're not getting started on the right foot. Take your time and think of it like dating because, with a successful company, you're going to be with this cofounding team for a while.

Celebrate: Enjoy the Journey

By taking those first few steps to turn your idea into action, you're braver than a lot of people out there. While you're just at the beginning of the adventure, make sure to pause to acknowledge your movement in the right direction. How? High fives, dinner out, a special reward—anything to help you honor the progress you've made. Honestly, it doesn't matter what the reward is—the acknowledgment is what matters.

For example, .CO Internet founder Juan Diego Calle took a moment to appreciate finding his first cofounder for .CO, Eduardo Santoyo. He recalls that they "celebrated that very moment together as the birth of a great partnership, although all we had at the time was an idea that had the chance to become a reality in the future."

Aside from celebrating your first milestones yourself or with a cofounder, consider sharing your progress with someone who has mentored or supported you up to this point. This not only helps you feel the progress but also communicates to your mentors that their time was well spent. Sapp of Fluencr used to talk about business with Baltimore Ravens majority owner Steve Bisciotti (a self-made billionaire), who often said that the hardest thing is just doing it. So Sapp made sure to phone Bisciotti to share the news after he took the first steps with Fluencr. "It felt good to call him up and say 'I took that first step, Mr. Bisciotti, and though I'm nowhere near my goals and dream, I at least took a step of faith in that direction,'" he recalls.

> ### .CO
>
> .CO is the domain name for innovators and entrepreneurs, with more than 1.6 million domains registered. The company also offers resources at go.co/members and a website builder at POP.co. .CO was launched in 2010 after founder Juan Diego Calle and his team won a bid from the Colombian government to administer it. Tech Cocktail is thankful to have .CO as a partner and supporter. Neustar acquired .CO in March 2014.

Final Thoughts

Early on, in brainstorming what she hoped BabbaCo would become, Kim knew that it was all about building relationships with customers, a lifestyle brand people would feel loyalty toward.

So it was a natural extension to develop the BabbaBox, a monthly shipment of activities for parents or caregivers to do with their kids. They solved a problem that many parents have: not knowing how to spend quality time with young children. They raised $1.25 million in funding in July, went through demo day at their accelerator in August, and shipped out their first boxes in September 2008.

Kim's company also built celebration into their weekly routine, making Wednesdays into Winsdays, where each team member shared their weekly progress. The Winsdays sessions focused the team on their small wins from week to week, helping everything from morale to company culture. In January 2014, BabbaCo was acquired by Barefoot Books. Kim says, "It's really this story of raw passion and following through with it" that made all the difference.

An idea that is developed and put into action is more important than an idea that exists only as an idea.

—Buddha

4 Formation

I have so much paperwork. I'm afraid my paperwork has paperwork.

—Gabrielle Zevin

You've taken the big step and started to turn your idea into a reality. There are a few things to consider as you embark on this journey. Eventually you'll need to make sure you actually create a company as a legal entity, understand what books you need to keep and forms you need to file, and have your tax details in order. These are probably not the first things you want to think of as you begin this exciting new chapter of life—and definitely not the most awe-inspiring tasks—but in my experience, the following items are very important not to gloss over in your formative months and years:

- Company formation
- Employee agreements
- Legal advice
- Bookkeeping and accounting
- Taxes

Why? Because no matter how great your company is, if your legal, financial, and tax affairs are out of control, they can have an enormously negative effect on your time, your sanity, and ultimately, the success of your company.

Let's dig into a few of these areas.

Forming a Company

A study by the entrepreneurship-focused Kauffman Foundation found that 60 percent of entrepreneurs worked on their idea for more than six months before actually forming an entity. Although forming an entity is not necessarily the first thing you need to do, when you finally do sit down to do it—with a lawyer or not—it makes sense to know your options. If you choose the wrong type, you'll have to spend more time and money reorganizing it later.

To start, here are some guidelines about entity types and which to choose. This information is readily available online, so I'm going to keep it concise here:

- *Sole proprietorship:* The setup is cheap and simple and includes registering for a business license and tax ID number. The downside is that you are personally liable for business debts.

- *Partnership:* Partnerships are similarly cheap and easy to set up; the only difference is that they include two or more people. You still have personal liability.

- *LLC (limited liability corporation):* An LLC is a pass-through entity: it doesn't pay corporate taxes, with the profits ending up on personal income tax returns. (This avoids double taxation, where the same amount gets taxed twice on business and personal returns.) You usually aren't personally liable (hence "limited liability"). An LLC is best if you don't plan to raise outside funding. Venture capitalists (VCs) typically won't touch an LLC because it exposes them to UBTI (unrelated business tax income) taxes and it's hard to work with the preferred membership units (the equivalent of shares) in LLCs.

- *S-Corp:* An S-Corp is also a pass-through entity. If you don't plan to raise VC money soon, you might choose an S-Corp because you avoid double taxation, there's no preferred stock, and it's easy to change to a C-Corp when the time comes. S-Corps come with regulations such as having a board of directors, issuing annual reports, and conducting shareholder meetings. Shareholders have

---

Kauffman Foundation

The Kauffman Foundation is a private foundation that was established in the 1960s by entrepreneur and philanthropist Ewing Marion Kauffman. The foundation focuses its efforts on education and entrepreneurship to encourage people to be economically independent and engaged citizens. Kauffman supports startups through its reports and research on entrepreneurship, resources at Entrepreneurship.org, and work with organizations such as UP Global. The foundation is based in Kansas City, Missouri.

to be U.S. citizens or permanent residents, and the profits (income) have to be divided among owners according to their share.

- *C-Corp:* A C-Corp is best if you're looking to raise outside funding in the near future. It's the most expensive option because of double taxation, but you do avoid the phantom income of LLCs and S-Corps, a phenomenon that occurs when you get personally taxed for your share of profits even if they were reinvested back into the business. C-Corps allow for preferred stock. Most startups choose to create Delaware corporations because of the friendly laws there.

- *B-Corp:* The B-Corp (benefit corporation) is available in a growing number of states and could be an option for your conscious company. It's really designed for for-profit companies that, in addition to driving profits, have a strong social good purpose and want to ensure they remain accountable and transparent in their actions.

- *Nonprofit:* For some startups with a social good mission, a nonprofit is the best choice. Nonprofits come with their own complex set of qualifying regulations and profit allocation rules, but they also have different benefits and opportunities. Not all social good startups are nonprofits, however.

I've found there are lots of opinions out there, even among the experts. So do your homework—read more about the various options, and talk to other startup owners, lawyers, and accountants. In the end, you're the one who will make the decision.

Also take the opportunity to register your trade name at the local city hall and get your business license.

Location

Where you base your company matters. I'm not talking about forming a Delaware corporation. I mean, literally, where are you going to live and set up shop? Realistically, most people start their company wherever they live. But it's still worth asking yourself the question—particularly if you live on a border of another area where setting up shop could have meaningful benefits such as lower taxes.

Seven states don't have state income tax: Alaska, Florida, Nevada, South Dakota, Texas, Washington, and Wyoming. Tennessee and New Hampshire have a limited income tax on individuals, taxing only dividend and interest income. So this is something to keep in mind.

Even if you work from home, just you and a laptop, you may need a home occupancy permit. It's easy, but you have to apply in person. You may need this to get your business license.

The strength of the startup community is another important factor to weigh as you look for funding, mentoring, events, and service providers to help you on your path. Silicon Valley has a drawn a lot of attention, but these days you can form a startup anywhere.

Employee Agreements

It's important to have a legal agreement between you and your cofounders. You, like many others, may think, "There's plenty of time to do that later. We don't even know if this startup will amount to anything yet." I've done it, and trust me when I say: it only gets harder. It's much easier to have all the difficult conversations early on. Equity, operational decisions, what happens if the company fails—make those decisions before everyone gets attached and emotional. There are not only personal challenges in waiting but legal and tax implications as well.

Company agreements may also include stipulations about duties, job descriptions, hours, how decisions are made, who pays for which expenses, what happens if you disagree about raising money or selling the company, whether you can launch other startups at the same time, and what happens if someone is injured or dies.

Your agreement should also specify what happens if cofounders or employees leave. If they own stock, can they sell it? Do other founders get first dibs? How is price determined?

Equity

You also have to decide how to split equity, either 50/50 or otherwise. Splitting 50/50 avoids arguments now, but uneven splits usually reflect the reality of each party's contributions.

Vesting

Vesting is a useful tool that helps ensure cofounders are in it for the long haul. When equity has a vesting schedule, team members earn the full rights to that equity over time instead of all at once. If equity is completely vested, it means it's completely owned by the team members. If they leave before a portion is vested, they don't receive it.

Steve Kaplan, counsel at Pillsbury Law in Washington, DC, advises startup founders to divide equity sooner rather than later. The tax implications of equity grants depend on the value of the company when equity is allocated, which is lower the earlier you do it.

Besides allocating stock to cofounders, you can also use stock as an incentive for employees. You can also award additional stock along the way at your discretion—for example, if a team member scores a huge deal or makes an outstanding contribution. This makes it a motivational tool as well as a reward for a job well done.

Intellectual Property

The most crucial thing you can do as you begin working with others is have them sign contracts stipulating that the company owns their work, says Daliah Saper of Saper Law in Chicago. Her firm focuses on intellectual property, social media, and business law, and they've seen what happens when founders forget to do this. For example, the following story is based on an actual client Saper had:

Marianne needed a website to start her business, and she hired Brad. Marianne paid Brad $60,000, because he's worth it, and Brad developed the entire site for her. There's no agreement in writing. Who owns the website?

Brad owns it. Just because a business pays for the work doesn't mean they own it; that's not how U.S. copyright laws work. You have to have a work-for-hire or assignment agreement in place that spells out whom the work belongs to. This applies to any freelancer—a videographer, photographer, Web developer, designer, and so on. Even independent subcontractors could end up being joint owners of the code because of copyright law.

Legal Advice

When choosing a lawyer, you're going to want someone whom you connect with and who can explain things in language you understand. Also remember that not every lawyer is right for every situation. You may have one lawyer who helps you with simple organization and business contracts, licensing technology, and writing your terms of service, but you may eventually need someone else if you get involved in complex patent situations, funding, or an acquisition. It's okay to use different attorneys for specific purposes, and typically your day-to-day lawyer can help make recommendations.

Bookkeeping and Accounting

Are you a numbers person? If so, you might like the accounting side of starting up a business. I don't. Either way, eventually you'll need to collect and spend money. One of the number one rules when starting a business is to *keep your personal and business financials separate*. Seriously.

We've all done it ... used a personal credit card to buy a domain name and hosting space or used a personal check to pay a contractor. In the earliest days, it might be unavoidable, but as soon as you really get serious about being a company, you need to get serious about your division of finances. This means you'll need to set up a bank account after forming your entity.

Once you start transacting as a business, you'll want to think about your bookkeeping and find a good accountant who has worked with startups. You'll definitely need an accountant and good record keeping skills if you plan to raise funding, because you'll have to show statements to banks, investors, and even friends and family if they contribute. You will also have to be up to date on all your state and local taxes.

Even if you aren't raising funds, good accounting will make it easier to make key decisions. It helps you understand revenues and expenses and figure out ways to optimize your business. Some of the elements of accounting include:

- A balance sheet, with assets and liabilities
- A list of account transactions
- An income statement, with revenue and expenses
- Payroll records
- Records of outstanding payments (that you owe and are owed)
- Taxes to pay during the year, if applicable

If accounting is new to you, then you may want to kick things off by meeting with an accountant to get an overview of what you should be tracking in your earliest months. Accountants can help you determine whether the business is fundamentally healthy or not and help you understand your tax landscape, liabilities, and obligations. Some local and state taxes have to be filed monthly or quarterly, for example, and unfiled taxes can result in fees, even if you had no revenue. And April 15 isn't the only tax date to be aware of; various forms and taxes are due at different times of the year.

To save yourself time and money, stay as organized as possible and don't use tools like QuickBooks if you don't understand them. A spreadsheet you understand will go so much further in helping you stay organized. A good bookkeeper will take care of all your general accounting duties on a daily or weekly basis. I advise you find one when you can afford it.

Be honest with yourself about how much you understand about your business, and either learn what you need to learn or bring in help via staff, a partner, or a professional service. For example, if you're running an e-commerce site and don't understand the terms *profit margin* and *cost of goods sold,* you'll have a very difficult time making the decisions you need to run the company.

For a list of tools for legal and accounting, check out http://tech .co/book.

The Harsh Reality

The recent films *The Social Network* and *Jobs* shine a light on some of the inner workings of business—and in business, there are sometimes cofounder troubles, disputes, and departures. In the Facebook lawsuit, the Winklevoss twins' ConnectU filed a lawsuit against Facebook. It was eventually settled for $20 million cash plus Facebook stock. Ousted cofounder of Snapchat Reggie Brown filed a lawsuit in early 2013 for one-third of the ownership of the photo messaging application developed by Stanford students.

Why does this happen? Lawyer Chris Good of Fowler & Good LLP has seen many startups struggle because they didn't clearly define things like roles and responsibilities. "This is fine if everyone is pushing the startup forward, but if someone starts backing away from the startup, this generally ends up either breaking up the company or in litigation," he says. Litigation is not what you want to be using your time, money, or energy on. Wouldn't you rather be focused on starting and running a company? So take our advice and clearly define your roles and responsibilities.

You don't necessarily need a lawyer to help you *make* decisions. Try to come to an agreement about key issues first and then find a lawyer to help paper the agreement so you have something to work off in the future.

When picking your lawyers and accountants, keep in mind that cheap is, well, cheap. SweatGuru chief executive officer (CEO) and cofounder Jamie Walker found that out the hard way when she selected the cheapest accountant available. After working with this individual for a while, she discovered the company wasn't even accredited. "It ended up being a nightmare and took us a good year and a half, a new accountant, and a lot more money, time, and energy to fix. They ended up screwing up all of our business tax information, which made our subsequent tax season extra painful and time-consuming."

When Jen and I set up Thankfulfor, we made a checklist of things we knew we had to do: set up our LLC, get a tax ID number, open a bank account, and more. But in the excitement of starting up, we didn't do enough research. When January rolled around, Jen reached out to an accountant, unaware of what was to come.

"Questions came pouring in. What is your state account number? Did you set up your sales tax account? Did you submit your Schedule K-1? Did you send out your 1099-MISC forms? Along with many others," she recalls. "My facade of organization came crumbling down." We spent the next few weeks bouncing back and forth between the tax offices at city hall, filling out forms, getting permits, and paying fees and fines. We got it all taken care of, but asking more questions up front would have saved time, money, and stress.

Celebrate: Enjoy the Journey

I'll be the first to admit that it's hard to make paperwork fun—but paperwork can be a lot of fun ... when you finish it. It's an amazing feeling when you know all your books are in order. One of the best things you can do is set up goals for getting your accounting and legal paperwork in order, and then celebrate. Set up a schedule—perhaps you do payments on Fridays and close out your books by the fifth of each month. Treat yourself to something you enjoy each time so you have something to look forward to.

Walker and her business partner at SweatGuru retreated up into the mountains to hammer out a business plan, investor deck, and financial documents. It took days, but they celebrated by returning to their families. Some apps are even making accounting fun by sending you push notifications when you receive money. Cha-ching!

Tech Cocktail lightens up an otherwise-boring employment contract by ending with this: "Despite the formality of this document, the Tech Cocktail team is jumping for joy, eating cupcakes (and green smoothies because we're health-conscious) at the prospect of you joining this team and helping to build this dream of ours into an amazingly awesome, new type of media company that will affect people around the globe!!!" To show their agreement, our employees are directed to sign and send a photo giving a thumbs up. And they actually do.

Final Thoughts

In the big picture of your business, paperwork may seem like a small but sharp nail hiding in the corner that you try to ignore as long as possible. But the more you learn, understand, and prepare, the less stress it will be, leaving you more time and energy to focus on your core business.

No matter how well prepared you try to be, there will be surprises. But your goal is to minimize them as much as possible. If you're considering starting a business, save yourself a lot of stress down the road and ask a lot of questions up front. Your mantra must be, "I don't know what I don't know—but someone else does." Use resources such as your local city, county, or state websites, where you can often find small business checklists of forms to fill out and taxes to pay.

I must end by sharing an important disclaimer: I'm not a lawyer or accountant and therefore this is not professional advice. I've made some suggestions and given you food for thought, but you'll still need to find trusted experts to advise you.

Part 2
Product

5 Product-Market Fit

In a great market—a market with lots of real potential customers—the market pulls product out of the startup.

—Marc Andreessen,
investor and cofounder of Netscape

In previous chapters, you've come up with ideas and started to turn them into action. You've simultaneously begun structuring your company as an official entity and pulling in the right people to help or advise you with accounting and legal (or at least started to think about it!). But now you've got to start testing your idea to determine whether it's something worth solving. You need to figure out who has the problem and what they're looking for to solve it. This will help you find your customers and, in doing so, lead to what's called product-market fit. The market should help guide you in the right direction.

You might say that inDinero, which makes software for account-ing, payroll, and taxes, was pulled out of the market by customers. It was cofounded by Jessica Mah while she was an undergraduate in com-puter science at the University of California, Berkeley. In the beginning, she asked herself: What's the most fun thing we can do to get this in the hands of customers? So inspired, she and her cofounder created mock-ups in Photoshop, pretending they had a product.

Small businesses were interested, so the team took it to the next level: they asked for credit card information. And more than 100 busi-nesses handed it over.

Mah knew a bit about the lean startup process, so she gave herself a strict schedule: every Friday, she would get out of the building and talk to customers. She would line up back-to-back interviews, meet customers at coffee shops, and then watch them use the product—the best kind of usability testing. "That was the smartest thing we did," she recalls in a Stanford Entrepreneurial Thought Leaders interview.

"Each customer led to a completely different set of insights that we wouldn't have gotten from past customers," she says. In the end, the best insights came from customers who fell somewhere in the middle—they didn't love or hate the product; they just liked it but saw a lot of problems.

Initially, Mah and her team thought they would build some kind of easier-to-use QuickBooks clone. But when they talked to small-business owners, they realized that businesses weren't using QuickBooks—and they didn't want to. They were using spreadsheets, and they wanted something simple and easy. Without talking to customers so systematically, inDinero would have created a product no one wanted—a solution without a problem.

As the inDinero story illustrates, you can have users before having product-market fit; the way to get there is to listen to them. And it takes awhile—a long process of patiently learning and revising and being humble. According to Ellie Cachette, vice president of product marketing at Koombea (previously founder of ConsumerBell), "There is almost a user for everything, so just gaining them is not always indicative of product-market fit. Product-market fit is defined by something that both has its niche but also has a supportive economy around it that is willing to pay. Some early disrupters take years to build up the use and the community around their product before reaching product-market fit."

Customer Development

It is easy to be heavy: hard to be light.

—G. K. Chesterton

Lean startup is a recent movement with origins tied to Eric Ries, an entrepreneur who coined the phrase in 2008. He was largely influenced by his startup experiences and learnings from his mentor Steve Blank, a Stanford University professor and entrepreneur. Blank calls Ries his best student.

Blank is known for advocating against the traditional product development approach—where you come up with an idea, develop it, test it, and launch it. With such little focus on your customers, you generally end up building something that no one wants, like inDinero almost did. As a result, Blank explains, companies that try to launch new products fail (that is, are not profitable) 9 out of 10 times.

Instead, Blank advocates for what he calls "customer development," which focuses on constant contact with customers. What does it look like? You figure out who your customers are and learn as much about them as possible. The job of the customer development team is to make sure that customers are interested in the particular features that are concurrently being built or learn their actual needs. Product development and customer development are happening at the same time and playing off each other.

When inDinero was young, everyone did customer development, going out to dinner once a week to discuss customer problems and decide on new features. Soon, they realized that their three- or six-month plans made no sense. Constantly learning about customers meant their product road map was constantly changing, so it was more reasonable to plan only a few weeks out.

To put this all into practice, you start with a very basic product created by the founders' vision. Then you identify some potential customers, and try to figure out how much they care about the problem you're focusing on. Ries calls this initial version a minimum viable product (MVP), allowing you to maximize learning with the least possible effort. Then, you test it. There's no marketing around these launches. They are simply tests. You can test with Google AdWords, landing pages, or paper prototypes (even before you have a product). The prototype hardly has to work, as long as it allows you to test the concepts you need to test and gather customer feedback and information.

For example, productivity and collaboration software company Twoodo created multiple landing pages, including different ways of expressing the problem and solution it was working on. Then, the team tested which ones had higher conversion rates, giving them insights into the real problems and needs of Twoodo customers. "The best strategy is still throwing pasta on a wall and seeing if it sticks," says Denis Duvauchelle, founder and chief executive officer (CEO).

weeSpring, now a community for sharing and finding baby product reviews, started out as simple as possible. The assumption the founders wanted to validate was that parents loved talking about baby products. So they created a survey on SurveyMonkey that asked only one question: "Which three baby products do you recommend to your friends most often?" weeSpring generated more than 500 responses in a few days with little promotion, and the founders considered their assumption validated.

What you're testing in this stage are the hypotheses you have about the problem, solution, customers, distribution, pricing, competition, and more. According to lean startup expert Ash Maurya, assumptions about the problem are often much riskier than assumptions about the solution. The solution would be risky if you were worried that you didn't have the technical capability to build it. But more often, you should be asking yourself things such as: Do people really have this problem? And will they actually pay to solve it?

Customer Validation

The second step in Blank's customer development is customer validation. To validate that your customers will actually do what you think they will do, you need to get people to purchase your product. And sometimes, the person purchasing isn't the same person who's using the product, as is the case for lots of business software. If you're on the right track, your customers and sales will be repeatable and scalable; in other words, you can use similar processes to acquire new customers. You need to be able to easily find more customers and make more sales; you don't want to run up against a wall where mainstream buyers aren't interested. If things aren't working, you may want to consider targeting a different group of customers or building a different product.

A little Chicago startup named The Point developed their first prototype for a new social e-commerce marketing concept on a simple WordPress site. But instead of taking off right away, traction was uneven. Customers flocked to one particular part of the site—where groups got together to negotiate discounts—and The Point eventually spun off that part into another little Chicago startup, Groupon, that quickly gained traction.

"Your idea is probably wrong," says Aaron Batalion, cofounder of LivingSocial. "Don't be scared, everyone pivots … there really are hundreds of pivots you go through as an entrepreneur."

Ries's lean startup methodology is also inspired by agile software development and lean manufacturing principles. It gives startups some structure to help eliminate uncertainties, rather than the haphazard guidance to just do it. Ideally, your first product is actually an experiment to answer the question, "Should this product be built?"

For a list of lean startup tools, check out http://tech.co/book.

Our Tech Cocktail journey has also been a process of testing, learning, and changing. A few years ago, I leveraged a white-label Ning product to build out a community site for Tech Cocktail with the goal of boosting online engagement around the brand. Registrations were strong, but activity was disappointing and got weaker over time. After our events, where were people creating profiles, connecting, and communicating? Facebook. I killed the Ning site and created a Facebook page for Tech Cocktail, which proved much more effective.

On the event side of our business, the market literally pulls our product into new geographic regions, which fuels our event expansion. The content side is trickier, and we constantly experiment to see what our audience responds to most in order to grow page views, return visits, shares, and newsletter subscriptions. Because of the highly competitive landscape, this part of the business is evolving at a rapid pace, requiring constant testing and monitoring.

If you're interested in finding out more about the lean startup methodology, I recommend you do some homework by reading Steve Blank, Eric Ries, and Ash Maurya. They wrote entire books on these concepts, and it's not my intention to rewrite their work. Some folks use lean startup methodology religiously, but you don't have to if you focus on your customers and in doing so, let that lead you to profitability and success.

The Harsh Reality

What happens if you don't listen to your customers (or even talk to them)? Well, you might spend a lot of time, money, and energy building an amazing piece of art that never sees the light of day or helps anyone.

Washington, DC–based startup Social Tables initially wanted to create a seating chart for weddings that was public and connected to Facebook profiles so that guests could see who else was at their table. But they didn't talk to customers until after launching the product and didn't do market research to see if there was competition. They launched and acquired 3,000 users, but none of them made their seating chart public—they just used it for personal reference.

Social Tables cofounder and CEO Dan Berger admits, "I did everything wrong. I didn't know what lean startup was ... I didn't know customer development, so I did every mistake possible in the book." Then, rather than talking to the customers about their problems, Social Tables spent a year and a half adding features the customers requested—eventually realizing that they had the wrong customers! They finally understood that it would be much more profitable to sell to big corporations instead of individuals, so they killed off their direct-to-consumer product.

Today, Social Tables is building meeting planning software for hotel catering teams and corporate meeting planners—a totally different business than what they started with. They used their customers as a course corrector to guide them to the enterprise space, after a few years flying blind with their own product development ideas and assumptions.

When Blake Hall started TroopSwap, the company was a daily deals site targeted at military personnel and veterans. But soon after launching, Hall and his team realized that brands were much more interested in how TroopSwap verified military identity. They had spent three months building a deals site when they could have used off-the-shelf, white-label technology and discovered the real problem faster.

"In the beginning … it's hard to parse the symptoms of a problem from its true root cause," says Hall. "We could have found product-market fit a lot faster." The story does have a happy ending: TroopSwap eventually evolved into ID.me, which handles identity verification of groups such as veterans and students for more than 60 national brands. And it won a $2.8 million grant for the president's National Strategy for Trusted Identities in Cyberspace.

TappedIn's story doesn't have such a happy ending. It was a Washington, DC–based startup cofounded by Zainab Zaki that was looking to create meaningful conversations at events via its application. If you knew more about attendees before or during an event, the founders thought, then you might be able to find people you wanted to meet and have more meaningful interactions. The idea had merit but, as Zaki explains, instead of talking to customers and launching an MVP, they spent more time on brainstorming, wireframing, drawing product road maps, and talking to investors, advisors, and peer groups.

She looks back and says, "If we had gotten the product out the door sooner, we would have collected valuable feedback and clear directions on where to take the product next. That was a huge mistake." After a few changes in direction and two and a half years, they reached the end of their road. "We struggled with finding product-market fit for the entire existence of our company. I would go so far as to say, not being able to find product-market fit was the primary reason we had to close TappedIn's doors," says Zaki.

The biggest issue for the lean startup methodology is its very popularity. These concepts are complex, and any summary (including this one) isn't comprehensive and nuanced enough to explain everything. Instead of blindly following the lean startup hype, take the time to educate yourself and figure out which aspects work for you.

Celebrate: Enjoy the Journey

That moment of truly finding your customers and product-market fit can be one of the most rewarding moments of the startup journey. Even if it's just the first meaty breadcrumbs on the path to real validation, this is an accomplishment to acknowledge! When Cachette was on the phone with her first client and they said, "I'd pay for that," she got them to prepay for a few months. "It was exciting," the Consumer-Bell founder explained, "because it's what investors were looking for (subscription-based revenue) but also it meant that we had a high bar set for losing them and had a couple months to really figure it out and provide excellent service."

And remember, you may have to refind your fit at multiple points throughout the life of your company as the market and competitors evolve or as you release new products. Enjoying this process is all in the approach and attitude you take.

For example, conducting customer development research and interviews doesn't have to be boring for either side. Colorado-based UrgentRx was working on turning typical over-the-counter drugs into fast-acting powders. To interact with customers, they wanted to make a big splash and differentiate themselves from staid pharmaceutical companies, without spending a lot of money, so they decided to get creative. Founder Jordan Eisenberg recounts:

> We have had a lot of fun playing the "Jester" brand and doing crazy stunts to disrupt the category. We've dressed large men up in tutus and fairy wings and dubbed them the "Pain Fairies" and had them running around New York doling out pain to people on the street. We had a blast interacting with people on the street, getting their feedback in real time, and creating a genuine connection with the public while telling them about our brand in a fun way. As a small startup, you have to be willing to shake things up and take calculated risks.

You can also create your own voice in your prototypes and carry that voice through everything you do. Customer development doesn't have to be something you dread. Use your creativity and have fun doing it; in the end it will help you stand out while you search for product-market fit.

Final Thoughts

inDinero's story might seem idyllic, but it really wasn't. While at Y Combinator, they decided they wanted to be the first startup from their accelerator featured in TechCrunch. So they went after press, got a ton of buzz, and saw some sign-ups. But it was too early for a big launch—people signed up, complained about bugs, and disappeared. Mah says she wishes they had waited longer, focusing on talking to early customers instead.

This experience and many others taught Mah that there's no such thing as an overnight success. Many times she thought the next release, the next launch, would be the thing that would rocket them to glory. But it never did. At some point, she reconciled herself to the fact that growth would be long and iterative and slow—she wouldn't suddenly have an epiphany about what her customers needed. She had to keep learning.

Still, she has an advantage over many startups—she loves her customers. Many entrepreneurs complain that their customers are unintelligent, not tech savvy, and clueless. Instead, Mah is happy to spend her days interacting with the small-business owners who use inDinero, who are entrepreneurs themselves. "I'm really proud to say that our customer base is really smart, really tech savvy. They get it, and they're really fun to talk to," she says. And according to Blank, that's a great sign.

6 Launch

The beginning is the most important part of the work.

—Plato

W hat is a product launch? Technically, it's the debut of your product or service to the world. Although I've orchestrated a number of launches of my own products, from startups to blogs to products at AOL for millions of users, I marveled at watching serial entrepreneur Tony Conrad launch his various products. His different launch styles should help set the stage for how to approach and eventually master the art of the launch.

Conrad invested in a company called Oddpost and its cofounders Ethan Diamond and Iain Lamb. Oddpost launched in 2002 as a Web-based e-mail product that leveraged Ajax to mimic a desktop e-mail client, revolutionary for its time as other e-mail services were primarily simple HTML interfaces.

To launch the product and gain exposure, the Oddpost team raised funding and hired a public relations (PR) agent to get them in front of journalists. They even paid $15,000 for a time slot on stage at a conference called DEMO to showcase their product. That was how you launched a product in 2003. In the summer of 2004, Oddpost was acquired by Yahoo! for an unconfirmed amount, rumored to be around $30 million.

Conrad's next product was Sphere, which he cofounded and launched in 2005. Sphere started out as a blog search that promised strong filtering and the best blog search results in the market. At the time, blog search was how you navigated the blogosphere, and Sphere was offering a better way to do so.

At this point, the launch techniques of 2003 no longer applied. Personal and professional blogs had changed all that. No longer did you have to pay $15,000 to get on stage to be in front of journalists at conferences like DEMO. You could approach bloggers like myself, Michael Arrington of TechCrunch, Om Malik of GigaOM, and Pete Cashmore of Mashable and get us to test out your product and (in some cases) use it every day.

To get people to try out Sphere, Conrad shared his product with as many bloggers and new media journalists as possible, then moved on to larger and more traditional publishers. Eventually Sphere was everywhere on the Web, powering the content recommendations of larger sites such as AOL, the *Wall Street Journal,* and GigaOM all the way down to the personal bloggers.

One of the lessons that Conrad learned was the power of personal bloggers and their social capital online. The blog post that stands out the most from Sphere's launch was not by TechCrunch, GigaOM, or the *Wall Street Journal* but on the personal blog of WordPress founder Matt Mullenweg. It was a simple post that said, "Sphere is cool, check it out." According to Conrad, Mullenweg's post had as much impact on Sphere's business as a TechCrunch article at the time. Sphere eventually changed its business to distributing content recommendation widgets on sites around the Internet and was acquired in 2008 by AOL.

A year later, Conrad was back at it with another startup. Once again, times had changed, and now you could launch a startup by leveraging the power of the social graph. With the launch of About.me, Conrad worked with 25 strategically selected advisors. These were people he wanted to be strongly associated with: folks like the current Twitter chief executive officer (CEO) Dick Costolo, Digg founder and now investor Kevin Rose, technology and gaming-centric video host Veronica Belmont, and more. Conrad asked himself, "Who's my posse? Who's my entourage?" And he launched his product with those people on his side: they created profiles on About.me and shared them via their Twitter profiles and e-mail signatures.

While About.me was still in beta, the influencer strategy worked and user adoption skyrocketed to hundreds of thousands of users. The product was quickly acquired by AOL just a few days after its public launch in 2010. It was eventually reacquired by Conrad and a group of other investors to give it additional life outside AOL. They've been iterating on it ever since.

Conrad's three stories illustrate how quickly the cost of launching a startup changed, as did the channels to launch. They also demonstrate some of the strategies used in successful launches. But nothing remains the same for long, and successful strategies must continue to evolve over time. You, like Conrad, must be able to recognize how things are changing and adjust to get your message out and build interest in your product.

Kickstarter

Launched in 2009 by Charles Adler, Perry Chen, and Yancey Strickler, Kickstarter lets you crowdfund your creative projects, such as video games, movies, apps, and technology. You set a goal, backers pledge money in exchange for rewards, and you have to meet your goal by the deadline in order to get funded. More than 55,000 projects have been funded successfully, for a total of $828 million. (The success rate exceeds 43 percent.) More than 50 of those projects have raised in excess of $1 million, led by the Pebble smartwatch (more than $10 million), OUYA video game console (more than $8 million), and *Veronica Mars* movie (more than $5 million). Kickstarter is based in Brooklyn.

One big change, for example, is that startups inspired by the lean startup approach are devoting less time and attention to a big, orchestrated, champagne-popping launch. You might just quietly launch your MVP, get feedback, and iterate, opting instead for a big announcement when you hit a large milestone. On Kickstarter, products "launch" before they even exist—they're just an idea in the founders' minds that needs some funding to get off the ground. So the tips in this chapter aren't just about the big launch—something that's happening less and less. The ideas of building community, timing, and good PR also apply to every big milestone in your company when you want attention: from launching to updating your app to hitting a big number of users to raising funding.

Launches and announcements are your opportunity to share your new baby with the world and to build interest and momentum. Media will give you only a limited amount of attention, so your goal is to get as much exposure as possible in that short period, building a strong foundation to grow upon rather than a momentary spike in interest. Here's what the process looks like.

Strategy

First, you need to think about what's right for your product and build a strategy. Are you a social product that needs to garner as many users as possible to gain any traction? Would your product, like About.me, benefit from having influencers involved in the rollout? Or do you have a marketplace that requires filling the supply funnel before you go in search of customers who will make purchases? Are you targeting businesses, which may require different tactics altogether?

There is no one-size-fits-all strategy around launching, so it's important to think about what your most important outcome of launching is, before the fact. You might find it's more important to solidify some big partnerships and then put a lot of PR power around announcing those deals. Or like About.me, perhaps it's a slow roll—building up huge usage and buzz during a beta period so that by the time you actually launch in the press—opening it up to anyone to use—you have thousands of users and a great story. In other situations, your primary goal might be simply generating huge awareness and getting as many mentions and links out in the press as possible. Or you might take the lean startup approach mentioned earlier.

The point is, put some thought into how you want to debut your product or service to the world. Think about the outcome you want and what you don't want. There are many ways to go about this, so be a student—look around at other launches and learn from them.

The following tactics are exactly that—just tactics. They're meant to get you thinking about the possibilities as you strategize about what's right for your company.

Launch Stages

You may have heard a startup being referred to as an alpha, private beta, or public beta product. Here's what those terms actually mean:

- *Alpha:* Very early and basic; bugs are still being worked out. Most alphas are private, tested only by internal employees or a small group of selected alpha testers.
- *Private beta:* The public, or a targeted group of users, can sign up, but someone needs to approve them before they start using your product. Google made the use of private beta mainstream by launching beta products like Gmail, which had an extraordinarily long beta period. In April 2004, it was invitation-only; a year later, users could sign up via SMS; the following year, some countries had open sign-ups; and finally, in August 2007, it was open to everyone. The popular Mailbox e-mail iOS app was briefly in private beta and showed you your number on the waiting list, which grew to 800,000 people long!
- *Public beta:* The product is still being tested, but anyone who signs up gets access. Public beta periods can be quite long and open-ended.

All told, your beta testing period should be on the order of magnitude of months, not weeks or years. After your public beta, you can eventually remove the beta label, indicating that the product is supposed to be higher quality and have fewer bugs. Some startups never make it out of beta, whereas others scrap all the labels and just go right for launch.

Build a Community

Testing phases are important to product development but also to your marketing, so think about how you communicate with testers—*they are your first community members.* Ask them for feedback to drive product improvements. That will help strengthen your connection with them, as they see that their ideas make a difference. These early-stage users are the ones you want to make advocates of your brand, and they will be important through the entire life of the product. After developing initial relationships with this community, you might ask them to help you spread the word.

Partners

The power of solid partnerships is something often overlooked by startups when they launch. Conrad did this through bloggers and other mainstream media distributing his Sphere widget across the Web. He did it with advisors who were social influencers during the launch of About.me. You can do it, too.

When thinking about launch partners, look for other people, products, or services that would benefit or complement your product offering. You might need to do some industry research to explore your options. Don't force it if it doesn't make sense, but if there's an obvious fit and benefit, it can be very advantageous. For example, Dwolla, a payment network that allows any business or person to send, request, and accept money, launched its new Dwolla Credit product with more than 40 partners in 2013 (more about that later). This was smart in not only building buzz but also demonstrating trust, which is critical when attracting merchants to new financial services.

Public Relations

Launch is an obvious time to start thinking about PR. Back when Odd-post launched, using a PR agency was how you got the word out—and many startups still think this way. If you're an early-stage, prerevenue startup with no funding, your limited dollars would probably be better spent elsewhere. To be totally honest, you can do it yourself. I'm not saying PR agencies are a waste of time for startups—they can be incredibly beneficial if you can afford it. If you get traction and funding, then you can bring on a PR agency to help you further spread your message.

The biggest reason to sign on a PR agency is to get very specific opportunities. For example, if you want to be on the *Today Show* or do a major television news show blitz, then you might need to hire an agency with the connections to make it happen. Relationships are one of the most important things a PR agency can offer you.

As you think about PR, start by doing some strategizing. Who is your target market? Who do you want to reach via press? Start by doing some research and making a list. Find out who writes about your industry, competitors, and related topics because they are more likely to write about you. As you think about press, consider everything from national mainstream publications to local media and topical blogs—anyone with an audience that you want to get in front of. Doing your homework here can really pay off.

You have limited time, so optimize it. Don't spend it pitching to a random trade publication that has nothing to do with your product or audience—it wastes their time and yours. If you're targeting stay-at-home moms, being featured in a slew of tech blogs is great, but you should also target the topical blogs that your customers actually read. Is your product a fashion product? Make a list of the top 100 fashion blogs and publications online and pitch to them.

Whether you pitch the product yourself or you use a PR agency, here's some advice on your pitch:

- *Keep it short.* Journalists are busy covering many stories.
- *Make it timely and relevant.* Help journalists with the angle and relevancy. Think about why people should care about your product in the context of their everyday lives. Figure out how it affects them positively and tell that story to reporters. Remember, if your story will get reporters a lot of page views, they'll want to tell it!

- *Don't send mass e-mails to reporters.* You're much more likely to get a reporter to respond to you if you connect with them one-on-one and make them feel special.

- *Iterate on your pitch* the way you iterate on your startup. Figure out which of your hypotheses may be wrong and test them. For example, you might believe that "journalists will open e-mails with 'sexy' in the subject line" but get zero responses when you try this approach.

- *Pitch early.* Allow for plenty of lead time so reporters can interview you and write a story without feeling rushed.

- *Most important, don't be arrogant.* No one wants to shine a light on someone who is arrogant, unless of course it is to show everyone else just what a jerk you are.

Build Relationships with Press

One of the best tips for dealing with reporters is to try to build relationships. Become a human being to them—not just a faceless sender spamming them with press releases—and they'll be much more likely to cover you. Reporters are people, not machines. Follow them on Twitter, and leave comments on their posts (not to the point of being annoying—find the right balance). Engage them, and find out how they like to be approached.

Once you've been covered, use a service such as Primeloop or just a simple spreadsheet to track your press mentions. Many startups display these on a press page on their website to add credibility.

The Harsh Reality

Launch time is exciting and can be a rush. But as much as you prepare and do your research, you have to be ready for the unexpected. Try to keep a level head; you'll need it to weather the storm.

Cheek'd is a New York–based dating startup that got on the cover of the *New York Times* Style section, which garnered lots of visitors and crashed their website. But even worse was a glitch on the back end that went unnoticed until after the fact. Cheek'd is a subscription-based business, and unfortunately its developer didn't flip the switch to store credit card information. Founder and CEO Lori Cheek shared that, "With hundreds and hundreds of new sign-ups, we lost nearly $30,000 in revenue from this simple mistake. I joke now that our London-based Web developer is lucky that he didn't live in America at the time." Although Cheek'd had a tough loss on opening day, a lesson was learned—don't let it happen to you.

More likely, your problem will be that you don't get very much attention around launch at all. Be prepared for that. Launching can seem like the end-all, but getting attention at launch is just the beginning. Now you have to go to work every day and keep your company going. Obsessing over launch is like obsessing over the wedding, then forgetting about the marriage part that comes next. Craig Bryant, founder of human resources management software Kin, agrees with me: "A product's initial launch is not the finish line," he says. "It's the starting line."

Celebrate: Enjoy the Journey

Launching an actual product people can use is not easy. It can take long hours and lots of sacrifices by the team. So once you launch, don't forget about the people who helped make the launch possible. Thank them with time off or rewards; figure out what your team cares about. For example, after Jason Calacanis and his team launched Mahalo, he took everyone to Disneyland as a reward. If Disneyland is too far, then try something nearby: dinner, a fun movie, a long weekend—anything to acknowledge the team's efforts.

You may not think of this one first, but also take time to celebrate with family or friends—since you've probably been neglecting them in the weeks or months leading up to launch.

Besides team and family, you can also celebrate with your community. For example, Las Vegas–based startup Tracky turned its launch party into a celebration of the Vegas tech community. They picked uniquely Vegas venues: the press event was at Switch's huge data center, and the party was at the former home of Mike Tyson, where part of *The Hangover* was filmed. Cofounder Jennifer Gosse shared, "What was most satisfying about the whole experience was the genuine sense of goodwill there. Everyone that I hugged and shook hands with that night expressed seemingly real enthusiasm about Tracky's launch. We've heard resoundingly good feedback about the deep sense of community and friendliness shared amongst then-partygoers, and now community members. And that, my friends, makes it an epic launch party to remember."

> ## Jason Calacanis
>
> Jason Calacanis was the cofounder of Weblogs (sold to AOL in 2005). He went on to start a variety of ventures, including the Mahalo search engine, ThisWeekIn podcast network, and the LAUNCH conference. Founded in 2010, LAUNCH now has a tech news site, podcast, and fund. The events attract thousands of attendees and allow startups to unveil themselves to the world. Based in Los Angeles, Calacanis is also an angel investor in startups such as Uber, Evernote, and Circa and founder of the stealthy startup Inside.com.

Final Thoughts

Although the art of the launch can be done a number of different ways, it's important to realize that the best *way* to launch a business is a moving target. Conrad launched three startups in a 10-year period, and each time he used a slightly different approach. Every business calls for a different launch strategy based on the customers the business is trying to attract. But the common denominator is usually relationships—relationships forged with the media, partners, and community.

7 Metrics

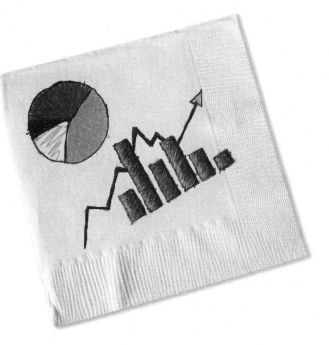

If there is not a metric [for it], it doesn't exist.

—Harper Reed,
chief technology officer of Obama for America 2012,
quoting Jim Messina, Obama's campaign manager

I n 2012, Uber had a math department that included two nuclear physicists, a computational neuroscientist, and a machine learning expert. Uber had launched in 2010 to provide on-demand rides to passengers, but it wasn't a transport company—it didn't own any sedans or taxis. Uber was in the business of logistics, and that requires lots of data.

Lots of different metrics matter to Uber. One is month-over-month growth, which hit 26 percent after about a year and a half. Uber also looked at the percentage of paying users who had paid in the last month, an indication that users were still active, not paying once and forgetting about the app altogether. Users are also active when the number of rides per rider per month goes up.

On the revenue side, Uber was interested in average revenue per person per month and average revenue growth in each city. As the company launched in new locations, it saw its revenue growth getting better and better—a sign that it was streamlining its processes and learning with each launch. The company also analyzed how much average revenue it was making on day 1, day 2, day 3, and so on, of a user's lifetime.

Uber used metrics to investigate assumptions—the service had worked in San Francisco, but would it work in other cities? Revenue growth said yes. Was Uber satisfying customers? The fact that customers were taking more rides per month looked promising. Metrics can help you test out ideas, track progress, and see how changes you make affect usage. Metrics are the symptoms of health or sickness in your startup baby, but not all new entrepreneur parents know how to understand them. This chapter will give you a primer.

Types of Metrics

One standard for startup metrics has been articulated by Dave McClure, the founder of 500 Startups. He calls them Startup Metrics for Pirates—AARRR:

- *Acquisition:* To acquire visitors on your site, you should focus on things such as advertising, e-mail marketing, search engine optimization (SEO), and public relations (PR). Think about which keywords are associated with your product, what your value proposition is, and how you compare to the competition.

- *Activation:* Activation metrics include things such as time on site, number of page views per visit, sign-ups, clicks, shares, downloads, and comments—in other words, users going from passive to active. You need to determine how much and what type of activity constitutes "active" for your product. Twitter was able to increase the number of people who finished the sign-up process (an activation metric) by tweaking it so finding people to follow was easier.

> ## Dave McClure
>
> Dave McClure is the founder and general partner at 500 Startups, an accelerator based in Mountain View, California. Founded in 2010, 500 Startups has invested in more than 600 companies, including Twilio, SendGrid, and Maker-Bot. It has a global focus, running invite-only trips around the world called Geeks on a Plane to learn about local startup communities. McClure is also a cofounder of StartupVisa.com, which mobilizes support for better immigration laws for entrepreneurs. Prior to 500 Startups, McClure spent time doing marketing for PayPal and Simply Hired and investing as an angel and a fund director.

- *Retention:* Retention means people come back, and a great way to drive retention is by sending e-mail reminders. From there, you can track open rates, click-through rates, percentage of those who come back, and frequency of visits. The metric you're trying to *minimize* is churn rate: the number of users who leave and never return.

- *Referral:* Users can refer your product through channels such as e-mail and social media. The typical advice is to aim for a viral growth factor greater than 1. Viral growth factor equals the percentage of users who invite others times the number of people they invite times the percentage who accept the invitation. In other words, a viral growth factor of 1 means every user is referring (on average) one other user to the service.

- *Revenue:* Revenue-based metrics include things like customer acquisition cost, the lifetime value of a customer, and the like.

In tracking all these types of metrics, focus on numbers that are actionable—those that actually have a bearing on your decisions. On Obama's 2012 reelection campaign, chief technology officer (CTO) Harper Reed and his team aggressively used metrics to help them take action faster. "Every time you had a conversation, you came with numbers that would back up your decision," says Reed. "You have to look at the numbers and say, 'Does this work?' You have to do it every single time." That approach helped them raise more than $700 million in online contributions.

Unfortunately, there are many metrics you could track that aren't actionable and have no bearing on your decisions. To avoid getting distracted by unactionable metrics, lean startup expert Eric Ries recommends that you hone in on these four types:

1. *Comparison metrics:* These metrics are derived from split testing (A/B tests), which allows you to choose one version over another based on which one performs better.

2. *Per-customer metrics:* Uber used average revenue per person per month. This is more valuable than tracking revenue, because revenue (hopefully) is always going up. But revenue can go up while average revenue per person per month goes down, which should set off a red flag.

3. *Keyword metrics:* These metrics track how users perform based on which keyword brought them to the site. Uber, for example, might learn that it earns more money from people who search Google for "private cars" than from people who search for "cheap taxis."

4. *Cohort metrics:* Cohorts are users who are grouped according to a certain characteristic. As lean startup entrepreneur Ash Maurya explains, you might separate cohorts by the date they joined, where they came from (Facebook or Twitter, for example), or their age. If the cohort of users who joined in March is performing way better than the cohort of users who joined in February, that might give you a clue that the new features you added in late February are popular.

Which Metrics Matter?

All this info is well and good, but which numbers should you actually be focusing on? This will be unique to your business and company stage. You need to look at your business and really hone in on what activities drive success. If it's getting users, track acquisition and referral metrics. If it's driving usage, track activation and retention. And so on.

The metrics you track also depend on your role in the business. If you're on the product development team, you want to look at conversion rates and see how the features you build affect them. If you're a marketer, you're looking for marketing channels that have a small price tag but high conversions—those that provide the most bang for your buck.

As you grow, expect your metrics to change. The metrics you use when you're validating a minimum viable product (MVP) will look different from metrics during launch and growth phases. For example, when you're trying to figure out which promotion channels are most effective, you may focus on conversion and churn rates. When you're validating your business model, you might focus on revenue per customer.

If you really believe in keeping things simple, listen to the advice of marketer Sean Ellis. He's known for advocating only one metric that matters until you hit product-market fit. That metric is 40 percent: getting to 40 percent of users who, when asked how they would feel *without* your product, respond with "very disappointed." Your job in the early stages, he says, is to do everything you can to increase that percentage. And in doing so, you'll be honing in on your product's must-have feature.

For a list of metrics tools, check out http://tech.co/book.

The Harsh Reality

As you've probably figured out by now, metrics are one of the more complicated ingredients of starting up a business. "Unfortunately, there are no universally relevant startup metrics. It depends what stage of development you're in, what your business model is, what your high-level goals are," explains Shanelle Mullin, director of marketing at Onboardly.

One of the big dangers with metrics is something called vanity metrics, those feel-good numbers that almost always go up, such as total users, page views, and downloads. You'll be tempted to focus on these metrics—and tell the world about them—but they don't usually say much about the health of your business. They're the opposite of actionable metrics.

For example, you might see that 75 percent of your users are still active. That sounds great! But if you look deeper and examine how many of those users signed up within the past month, you might notice that all of them did. That means that everyone who signed up earlier has stopped using the app: you have horrible retention. Bragging that you have, say, 10,000 active users or 75 percent active users makes the situation sound much better than it is.

My cofounder and COO Jen Consalvo knows firsthand how easy it can be to get overexcited when you first launch and see an initial usage spike. When we worked at AOL, it was common to have a new product featured on the AOL Welcome Screen—also known as the firehose—and see your traffic numbers soar. "I quickly learned that it's when the firehose stopped that the real test began," Jen recalls. "Did people go back after they left? Did we create the right level of product 'stickiness,' as we used to call it, to get them to want to return? Or mechanisms to pull them back in or remind them? Did retention decrease or increase over the coming weeks? Who were our core users—the ones who used the product religiously—versus our casual users, and why?" If you suspect that initial traction is inflated as a result of lots of press or some other reason, remember that the number will likely drop before it stabilizes.

That's why it's really important to figure out which metrics matter and start paying attention to those instead. If you're a beginner to metrics, beware. "Vanity metrics are the metrics that make you feel good about yourself and that make you feel successful, but they just cloud your judgment," says Mullin. "You won't know you're stagnant or worse until it's too late."

Celebrate: Enjoy the Journey

Hooman Radfar is an expert on metrics. He's the cofounder and chairman of AddThis, which builds social plug-ins and analytics for publishers and advertisers. AddThis has grown to more than 14 million sites, reaching 1.6 billion unique users per month.

Early on, AddThis thought that celebrating too much would mean it was being complacent. But the team soon realized that celebrating metrics—such as how many users they were reaching and how much revenue they were making—could boost everyone's motivation.

"If people can celebrate along the way, you can transform something (which has to be a sprint by definition if you're trying to build a half-a-billion- or a billion-dollar company) into a marathon—where it's fun, there's something to look forward to, there's always new challenges," says Radfar. Metrics are an easy thing to celebrate because they're tangible; they lend themselves to milestones such as 100 this or 10,000 that.

"I remember when I first started at AOL," my cofounder Jen recounts, "and we had just hit 5 million paying subscribers, which was an enormous feat. All of a sudden, all my colleagues received these really cool AOL leather jackets. They were quick to tell me that when they had hit an earlier milestone (I think around 2 million paying members), CEO [chief executive officer] Steve Case promised all current employees he would buy them a jacket if they could hit 5 million. It didn't take long. Employees wore their jackets all the time—it was a serious badge of pride."

On Fridays, Tech Cocktail sends out a newsletter with our top articles and videos from the week—and sees a spike in traffic as people receive the newsletter and click over to our site. I decided to make this a fun, weekly ritual and celebrate readers reading Tech Cocktail! I project Tech Cocktail site traffic onto our big-screen TV in the office, encourage our remote team to pull up the real-time analytics dashboard online, and announce that it's time for the traffic dance! This brings joy to our editorial team as all the hard work from the week culminates in a traffic spike.

Whenever Mullin of Onboardly hits a milestone—such as reaching 10,000 unique visitors to their content marketing and PR blog—she and her team celebrate, talk about why they succeeded, and set a new goal. "It's important to celebrate the small wins, especially with startups," she says. "It's a long road."

Final Thoughts

Metrics are the vital signs of your business, and every startup has a different way to measure its health based on what it's trying to accomplish. The key is to focus on the metrics that matter and really move the needle for your goals, rather than getting blinded by numbers that give only the appearance of progress. So dig a little deeper to find your metrics. Once you do, you'll have found your compass—one that can help motivate you and your entire team toward startup success.

Part 3
Team and People

8 Team

Alone we can do so little; together we can do so much.

—Helen Keller

W hether you're a startup founder or running an existing business, you're tasked with building an amazing team that will go to battle with you and dig deep in the trenches for long hours, every working day of the year. You will interact with these people more than your family—some may even be family! *This group of A-player, determined individuals will be the ones to help you realize your vision.* But ... here's the deal. *It's not that easy to build an amazing team.* Here are some things I've learned along the way through my own experience and from other founders.

What to Look For

- *Attitude:* FeedBurner was a Chicago-based startup that created the equivalent of the plumbing for the syndicated Internet: a platform for powering content feeds across the Web. It was founded in 2004 by Dick Costolo, Matt Shobe, Steve Olechowski, and Eric Lunt, and after raising $8 million in funding, FeedBurner was acquired by Google for $100 million.

  Lunt was the chief technology officer (CTO), tasked with building the technology team. Lunt believes it's the *relationship of the founding team members* that helps build the foundation for future hires. He also believes there are a couple types of hires—he buckets them into specialists and best athletes. Specialists tend to be high-profile salespeople with a Rolodex or amazing marketing people, and they're expensive to hire.

  Therefore, in an early-stage startup, Lunt recommends bringing on best athletes (or stem cells), meaning people who are great at lots of things. I agree, and here's why. When you have 7 to 12 employees, you're going to have a flexible, flat organizational chart. Employees will have their specific roles, but they will each have multiple roles to perform, too. Everyone will be hustling to keep the company going in the right direction. Every few weeks or months, there will be different obstacles that come your way—and you will need highly flexible, self-motivated people to attack these problems head on.

Everyone on the team should feel empowered to take things on, as needed, even if it's not their job. If you're hiring specialists, this type of mentality may be foreign to them. Some may believe it's not their responsibility, because it's not in their job description. This is toxic to the culture of a startup.

- *Talent:* If their attitude is right, the next thing to look for in potential employees is talent. In the words of Napoleon Dynamite, "Girls only want boyfriends who have great skills." One way to test skills is to have potential hires do some kind of test project first and get paid for it. This allows you to try before you buy. You can do this with short-term projects or even longer-term ones, bringing people on as contractors first and, if you like them and their work, eventually hiring them full-time. I've done that quite a bit, with many members of the team either doing test runs or working as contractors first. If things don't work out, it's much easier for everyone to end a contract than to terminate employment.

  Michael Chasen, the cofounder of Blackboard and now founder of SocialRadar, hires people who are more than qualified for their current roles so that they'll be able to grow quickly into new roles. "Remember as a kid, your parents would buy you a winter coat one size too big so it would fit not only this season but next? They were on to something," he says. "You want people who will not simply settle into a limited role in the present but who will help the company get to the next phase as soon and smoothly as possible. It's not hiring people who are overqualified. It's hiring people whose qualifications will become more relevant with each passing week."

- *Culture:* Throughout the process, keep an eye on culture fit. Lunt is the first to point out that the first hires have a huge impact on the company culture. "Think about the percentage of influence to the culture of the company that those first employees have.

While the founders still have a heavy influence, the rest of the team is going to also set the tone for everyone else after them. So you really need to screen for cultural fit," he says. I'll talk more about culture later.

- *Personality:* Besides attitude, skills, and culture, start thinking about the personality traits you want your early employees to have. You might want people with drive or empathy, people who are team players or outside-the-box thinkers, or people who are positive and responsible. It's up to you. But one thing is nonnegotiable: being passionate for the company and mission. The chief operating officer (COO) of Boston-based startup Jebbit, Jonathan Lacoste, explains, "If you find someone [who] has a burning desire every morning to change the world, it'll do a world of wonder for team motivation and chemistry. You'll find that these are the people that 'wow' you on a regular basis and become advantages against your greatest competition."

Who to Hire?

In the beginning, many startup founders find it easiest to work with friends, family, and anyone else who is as passionate as they are about the project. These are people they trust, whose personalities and motivations are known.

Put some thought into the roles you give your family and friends and the expectations you set. If you become successful, will they expect to have a senior leadership position in the company? Do you think they can grow along with you? If you know you might eventually have to replace them or hire managers for them, would it put you in a tough spot? These are all questions that various entrepreneurs have had to face.

During your early days, you may be bootstrapping and working with freelancers, contractors, and fans of the project. You'll want to stay as lean as possible for as long as possible and hire only when it makes sense in terms of cash flow and business goals. You may all have too much work to do, but does hiring a marketer actually increase your revenues? In a post called "Lean Hiring Tips," lean startup expert Eric Ries advises not to hire anyone unless you've tried and failed to do the job. The reason is because trying to do it yourself has three possible (all good) outcomes: (1) you'll discover you and your existing team can't do it, but you'll get an appreciation for the task; (2) you'll discover your team can do it; or (3) you'll discover that you can do it but it's not crucial.

At some point, though, you'll need additional help. Everyone has a different take on the first positions you need to hire, but it really depends on your industry and company. Steve Blank believes you need a hacker, hustler, designer, and visionary (although one person can do multiple things). Within a small team, everyone can help with marketing, especially in this day and age of social media. Your core team will also be doing business development for the early stages of the company and, to be honest, wearing many other hats, too. You probably don't need in-house human resources (HR), legal, or accounting employees because they can all be easily outsourced and are too expensive to have on staff. Again, your startup will have its own needs.

Once you get past the initial bootstrapping days (which in reality can be months and even years), you can start to bring some of your contract employees on full-time and find more qualified people that you can now afford. It's an evolution, because a startup is literally in a constant state of change.

Outsourcing

The most likely candidate for outsourcing in tech startups is the development team, but it could include other key roles like design or HR. There are pros and cons to both options. Let's start by talking about development/production outsourcing.

On the positive side, outsourcing is usually cheaper. It's helpful for tasks or skills that you aren't an expert at—and if you're a businessperson who can't find a tech cofounder, outsourcing can sometimes be necessary. Skype, the hugely popular voice over Internet Protocol (VoIP) app, was founded in Sweden but originally created by developers in Estonia. Digg, the community news site, was created by a programmer from the outsourcing website Elance. AppSumo, the daily deals company, was built in a weekend for $60 using an outsourced team from Pakistan. Outsourcing can be relatively inexpensive and shockingly fast. On the negative side, whomever you outsource to is less invested in your business than a cofounder or employee would be, because outsourcing companies have multiple projects. And if you outsource key roles, it may be harder to create an integrated company culture.

When it comes to other types of outsourcing, such as HR, accounting, and legal services, I'll reiterate that most early-stage startups should outsource. Whether it's finding a local lawyer or accountant to work with on an ad hoc basis or working with a professional employer organization to manage payroll/taxes and benefits, you'll want to benefit from the best experts out there and leverage their resources as much as possible. Talk to others in your local tech community, and ask for recommendations.

For a list of hiring tools, check out http://tech.co/book.

The Harsh Reality

Sometimes you end up hiring people who aren't a fit—people who don't deliver or work against the team spirit and culture you're trying to build. You know it deep down, lose sleep, don't know how you let it happen, and don't know what to do about it.

I don't like firing people—no one does. Well, maybe Donald Trump does. But in real life, it's not quite what Donald Trump makes it out to be. It generally sucks, but as the boss, you gotta do what you gotta do.

Chris Dixon, an investor at Andreessen Horowitz, writes this about firing: "You're in control of a situation that will meaningfully hurt someone. It's an awful place to be. The fired person will go home and tell his/her family about how terrible it was. It was your fault. Perhaps your mismanagement caused it. Who knows. You'll question it, and perhaps you are right to do so."

It's easy to delay the firing process, rationalizing to yourself that the person is getting some work done and maybe he or she will improve. SweatGuru felt this way early on: the founders had hired their friends, and it took awhile to realize that they needed to start over with a whole new team. "Unfortunately, we didn't move fast enough to remedy the situation," recalls founder and chief executive officer (CEO) Jamie Walker. "We loved the personalities on our team and were reluctant to part with them."

> **Chris Dixon**
>
> Chris Dixon is a serial entrepreneur and investor who's now a general partner at the venture capital firm Andreessen Horowitz. In 2005, he cofounded SiteAdvisor, a consumer security company, and it was acquired by McAfee in 2006. His recommendation engine Hunch (founded in 2007 with Caterina Fake) was acquired by eBay in 2011. On the investment side, he started the Founder Collective venture capital firm and invested in companies such as Group.me, BuzzFeed, and MakerBot. As an angel, he has personally invested in Kickstarter, Foursquare, Pinterest, and more. Dixon is based in New York City.

Let's say your bad hire is a salesperson. What harm will that do? Even worse than building bad code, a bad salesperson can alienate potential clients. This person could poison the well for your brand for quite a while by stressing or severing relationships, negatively affecting your image. Once the well is poisoned, it might take you weeks, months, or even years to get back in front of the same company or customers.

This is the reason why hiring your friends and family can be tough: you might have to let them go at some point.

In addition, *you* might be fired once you have investors and a board. Steve Jobs was famously ousted from his CEO role at Apple in 1985. In his Stanford commencement address, he recalled the painful experience: "At 30, I was out—and very publicly out. What had been the focus of my entire adult life was gone, and it was devastating. I really didn't know what to do for a few months. I felt that I had let the previous generation of entrepreneurs down."

Even if no one's getting fired, team troubles are some of the gnarliest to untangle. It's an unfortunate fact of life that some of the most brilliant people are also divas or jerks, and you'll be tempted to hire them and convince yourself it's worth it. It's usually not: they are a drain on morale and productivity.

> ### Robert Scoble
>
> Robert Scoble, also known as @Scobleizer, grew up in Silicon Valley and has always been obsessed with new technology. He's currently the startup liaison for Rackspace, seeking out young startups Rackspace might like to work with. He also blogs about startups and is known for his forward-thinking predictions (some of which you can read in his latest book, *The Age of Context*). Previously, Scoble worked as a strategist at Microsoft and ran FastCompany.tv.

Netflix calls this type of people "brilliant jerks," and part of their culture is to not tolerate them. Thought leader Robert Scoble says, "The thing that destroys companies is hiring assholes. Looking for interesting people who are also nice is key at a big company." Whatever you call this breed of employee, beware—they bite. Cindy Gallop, the founder of IfWeRanTheWorld and MakeLoveNotPorn, says this about the people she hires: "They have to be extraordinarily brilliant at what they do, but they also have to be very, very nice people. Great and nice is my hiring philosophy—you cannot have one without the other. You can't be brilliant and not a team player and able to work with, motivate, and inspire everybody else around you."

But even nonjerks sometimes don't get along. Management expert Scott Berkun believes that most teams suffer from one of four problems: a lack of trust, old wounds, conflicting priorities, or poorly defined goals. Solving these problems sometimes requires you to reorganize your team, change your goals, or stop a project altogether. And the harsh reality is that team problems can often be traced back to poor leadership. "No one can lead a team well if they've never been on a good team. [And] many people never experience a good, healthy team," he says.

Berkun recommends interviewing team members when something is wrong and asking about their frustrations. "If none of them involve you, you haven't heard the whole truth yet," he says.

David Hassell, founder and CEO of 15Five, learned this at his previous company. They started seeing a high turnover rate and weren't sure why—until Hassell realized it was his fault. He and his partner had conflicting values, and they had each hired teams that agreed with them, slicing the company in half. "This made an absolute mess of our company's culture," he recalls.

Outsourcing is a whole other can of worms—it doesn't always work out the way you think it will. Although there are a number of reputable services out there, there are hundreds more that give outsourcing a bad rap. Jinesh Parekh, the CEO of Idyllic Software, warns, "When you are not their important client, you will be allocated the mediocre hires, and that can hamper your business in big ways."

Cindy Gallop

Born in the United Kingdom in 1960, Cindy Gallop grew up in Brunei and came to her entrepreneurial career from the advertising world, where she worked with brands including Coca-Cola, Polaroid, and Ray-Ban. Her Twitter bio reads, "I like to blow shit up. I am the Michael Bay of business." After a sort of midlife crisis, she became an entrepreneur and launched MakeLoveNot Porn at the 2009 TED conference. The company has grown to a team of eight and in 2012 launched MakeLoveNot Porn.tv, where people can view, share, and make profits on their real-world porn. Gallop is also the founder of IfWeRanThe World, a site that brings people and companies together to take small actions on their causes.

This is the Harsh Reality section, so I'm about to get personal. Before we took on Tech Cocktail full-time, Jen and I came up with a plethora of ideas. Thankfulfor was one of them, but there was another side project near and dear to our hearts, code-named The Willow Road Project after the road that now crosses Hacker Way in Silicon Valley. Willow Road was a video startup focused on community. We outsourced it all to get a first version out the door, thinking we'd hire a full-time team later once we started to bring in revenue or took funding. Looking back, we felt very excited and organized but ultimately made every mistake in the book—and it cost us.

The overseas development group that we hired kept swapping out people, didn't like phone calls, and were difficult to communicate with. We should have driven the schedule and made the payments based on actual delivery milestones. We didn't. We let their project manager take the wheel much of the time. We did continuously test and give feedback, but we just never made the progress we needed to make.

When we finally decided to pull the plug (because we realized it would be a costly endeavor—probably a long road that would require significant funding), we had already spent around 20,000 of our hard-earned dollars. *Pulling the plug was the right decision.* The mistake was that we never demanded the code that was already written. We asked for it, but they never gave us an answer and we just let it go, opting to move on to our next venture. To be fair, it would probably be useless now and we'd start over anyway, but the point is that we paid for it and never got it.

I don't like thinking of that project because I still love the concept and would handle it so much differently today (and hope to someday). On the bright side, we took a chance and learned a lot about what not to do on future projects. If any of the preceding description looks like something you are in the middle of, take control now.

Celebrate: Enjoy the Journey

Celebrating your team means celebrating people, so this shouldn't feel like a chore. And it all starts the minute you hire someone.

John Genovese of PolitePersistence lets the new hire pick a place for dinner. "They have something to look forward to and the team can let their hair down and get to know each other in a more informal environment before they get thrown into the fire," he says.

For your existing team, get-togethers and retreats are a great time for celebration. 15Five does a retreat every quarter, where everyone has fun, bonds, and celebrates their progress. "Health and vitality are values we share, so we always make it a point to get fresh air, get active, and have a blast," says Hassell. One time they went skiing at Lake Tahoe; another time, they rented ATVs and drove through the Red Rocks in Arizona.

Although we have talked a lot about the ups and downs of outsourcing, you can also make outsourcing fun for everyone involved. Parekh of Idyllic Software likes to treat outsourced or contractor employees as part of the team. He says, "Instead of thinking to bargain the last bit out of them, focus on ensuring you are their most important client. Pay well and get awesome work done from them. When you consider them to be a part of your team and pass on small tokens of appreciation, it goes a long way. When they hit a milestone, go take them out. If you are offshoring, go get yourself a vacation and work with them. This ensures you know them at a human level rather than just a financial level. Celebrate just how you would with your team."

Liam Martin, cofounder of Staff.com, is also a master of managing remote teams (he rarely sees his team members in person). He has a similar idea for outsourced teams: do social activities together and share your lives outside of work. For his team, he facilitates group Skype chat rooms, video messages for birthdays, and holiday parties around the world (three or four in different cities). Sometimes, they even pay for everyone to fly to a central destination and spend time celebrating together.

The Basecamp team works remotely and has chat rooms set up for ongoing conversations about the team's array of interests, from films to dogs. This keeps the conversation flowing and ultimately keeps everyone collaborating regularly—and it could work for outsourced teams as well. Bringing your team closer together is key.

Final Thoughts

Ask any entrepreneur or startup founder to list the most important success factors that go into building a startup, and many would put team at the top of their list. No one builds a company by themselves, so your success hinges on being able to build and manage your army. Finding the right team members, being thoughtful about processes and communication, asking for feedback, and treating people with respect play a foundational role in establishing a strong team.

9 Culture

To win in the marketplace, you must first win in the workplace.

—Doug Conant,
Campbell Soup

My first job out of college was at an upstart consulting company. The team of engineers was small, scrappy, and youthful, and there was a strong sense of family-driven company culture. We worked closely together and (as consultants) also traveled together to see clients, so we spent some days, weeks, and months on the road. That led to solid relationships, which turned into regular activities outside the office, such as bowling, happy hours, and open mic nights.

The office had a foosball table, and the team would take breaks to blow off steam while challenging one another to some rather intense matches. The company also organized an annual baseball game outing in the summer and a ski trip in the spring that the entire company attended, staying in one huge house together. Every quarter there were company meetings to shine a light on everyone's latest work and successes in a fun-infused environment.

This was my first impression of a strong company culture. It turned my place of work into a place I wanted to be and a place I looked forward to going every day.

Fast-forward to today, and I'm now working out of the mecca of company culture—Las Vegas, home to Zappos. Led by chief executive officer (CEO) Tony Hsieh, Zappos turned to culture to ensure that employees wouldn't wake up one day and not want to go to work, which is what happened to Hsieh at his previous company, LinkExchange.

During the Internet boom in 1996, Hsieh cofounded LinkExchange, an early ad network. At first the founders hired friends who wanted to be part of something exciting, but then LinkExchange got funding and started hiring very fast. They hired "any warm body who was willing to work for us and hadn't done more than six months of jail time," Hsieh recalls in the book *Delivering Happiness*. "We simply didn't know we should have paid more attention to our company culture." By 1998, the company had grown to more than 100 employees.

"One day," recalls Hsieh, "I woke up after hitting the snooze button on my alarm clock six times. I was about to hit it a seventh time when I suddenly realized something. The last time I had snoozed this many times was when I was dreading going to work at Oracle. It was happening again, except this time I was dreading going to work at LinkExchange. This was a really weird realization for me. I was the cofounder of LinkExchange, and yet the company was no longer a place I wanted to be at." So when Hsieh got involved with Zappos, he knew he couldn't let that happen again.

Hsieh was an early investor in Zappos as part of a fund and incubator called Venture Frogs. In the early days, Zappos struggled. Hsieh started putting his own money into Zappos to keep it going, and around 2000, he finally decided to work on it full-time. Zappos survived the dot-com crash and was successfully making money, so management started focusing on customer service.

After moving to Las Vegas, Zappos started devoting its attention to company culture. Management felt that customer service would fall into place if the company culture were solid. Based on their six years of experience, they created 10 core values that bubbled to the surface:

1. Deliver WOW through service.

2. Embrace and drive change.

3. Create fun and a little weirdness.

4. Be adventurous, creative, and open-minded.

5. Pursue growth and learning.

6. Build honest and open relationships with communication.

7. Build a positive team and family spirit.

8. Do more with less.

9. Be passionate and determined.

10. Be humble.

From then on, Zappos used these guiding principles for everything it did, including hiring for culture fit. Now, each potential hire goes on one full interview for culture fit and faces specific questions related to each of the core values. Zappos also created a four-week training program that has new recruits do two weeks of customer service calls. After training, they offer to pay a new hire $2,000 to quit. This is a litmus test to ensure that everyone really wants to be at Zappos. And it works.

Once people are hired, they start getting to know their coworkers. To help facilitate employee interactions in their old office, Zappos made sure there was only one door to enter the building. At one point, signing on to your Zappos computer actually required you to guess a fellow employee's name based on a photo of his or her face.

Zappos recognizes that culture is always changing. Management regularly surveys employees about their feelings of purpose and happiness at work. The Zappos Core Values Document challenges everyone to make one improvement a week to make the company better reflect its cultural values—something as simple as rewriting a form to be more accurate or fun. That way, everyone in the company is constantly working to improve the culture.

Zappos is part of a recent movement emphasizing the importance of company culture in employee happiness and productivity. According to RoundPegg, a Boulder, Colorado–based company that makes apps to grow your culture and engage employees, companies where employees are culturally aligned are six times more profitable than their competitors. RoundPegg has also found that culture explains 89 percent of whether an employee will thrive or fail in an organization. Yet only 42 percent of employees know their company's vision, mission, and cultural values, according to a 2013 survey by a startup called TINYpulse.

Although I learned some early lessons about culture from my first job out of college, I've learned even more from Tech Cocktail. Our team has primarily worked remotely for years, spread across several time zones, creating a slightly different kind of company culture. To ensure there are richer interactions, we spend more time seeing each other on video chats with Google Hangouts, Skype, or FaceTime. We also try to get employees to go to actual, physical events so our team can meet each other and interact. You learn a lot when you understand another human being's tone, interaction, and body language.

Even with all the technology available today, it's still especially important to spend time with your team in the flesh. You will learn a lot, form a better bond, and build better culture. It's much easier to work from afar once you have that baseline understanding.

Aside from the fun activities you can do with your team, culture is about creating a guide to what you want to be. It's about values and habits. It's a road map for how to hire and interact as a team and with your customers. If you can nail this, your company should be able to operate better without asking the cofounders 21 questions every time a unique situation arises. A team that understands the culture can have more autonomy because everyone has a framework for making decisions.

Figuring Out Your Culture

Not every company is the same. You and your team can (and should) choose your values. How do you do this? Ask your employees, because you probably already have the groundwork of a culture, even if it isn't formalized. You can't just pull a culture out of thin air; you have to figure out what it *is* before you can go about making incremental changes.

Manpreet Singh, president and chief operating officer (COO) of Seva Call, says:

> Your team members have distinct job histories and personalities. Each comes to the table already behaving according to the unique corporate culture he or she has adopted over the course of that

person's career. As a result, early-stage startups are often staffed by strangers who speak different languages in a way, holding competing assumptions and expectations of one another. They're like immigrants from vastly distinct countries and cultures coming together to found a new world. The goal, then, is not to merely create a culture, but to integrate the most effective aspects of the cultures people bring into the office.

When coming up with your core values and the foundation for your company culture, you should also think about your product. What values does your product promote? It works best if they're aligned with your cultural values. Here is a simplistic example: the events that Tech Cocktail hosts (which are part of our products) are fun, quirky, and educational, and so is our culture.

How many values should you create? That's up to you. There's no right or wrong answer, but you want to make sure each value makes sense to your business. Too many core values could be overwhelming to live by as a company, and too few might not cover everything you want in a culture. Zappos has 10 core values. RoundPegg recommends you pick three to five.

Here are some examples of core values that other companies have in place:

- *Eventbrite:* Eventbrite is accessible, empowering, delightful, dedicated, innovative, and genuine.
- *HubSpot:* HubSpot is maniacal about mission and metrics and unreasonably picky about team members. They believe in solving for the customer, being radically transparent, giving themselves the autonomy to be awesome, investing in individual mastery and market value, and questioning the status quo.
- *Netflix:* At Netflix, values are what they value, not what they say they value. They believe in high performance, freedom and responsibility, setting the context for good work but not controlling the

people you manage, being highly aligned but loosely coupled (that is, aligned on goals but free to come up with different strategies and tactics), paying top of market, and offering opportunities for progress and self-improvement.

- *Twilio:* Twilio believes in living the spirit of challenge, empowering others, starting with why, creating experiences, not tolerating shenanigans, being humble, thinking at scale, "drawing the owl" (figuring things out for yourself), and being frugal.

Tech Cocktail's values are:

- Celebrate uniqueness and value authenticity and personal growth.
- Do more with less and always try to have fun while doing it.
- Own your stuff and strive for excellence.
- Be autonomous, but collaborate and err on the side of inclusiveness.
- Be humble yet positive.
- Value health and personal life.
- Be passionate and determined about what we do and compassionate and encouraging with others.
- Stay flexible and open minded; be experimental with a spirit of innovation.
- Great communication, integrity, and trust will be our strongest foundation.
- Celebrate to motivate!

Living Your Culture

The problem with lots of company cultures is that they stay confined to a list of values on the wall or on a website. If you really want to live your culture, here are a few things to think about.

Your own personal behavior as a founder or team member influences the company culture. In a previous chapter, we discussed how Eric Lunt experienced firsthand the importance of company culture and the influence of the first few employees on it.

Like Zappos, consider culture fit when hiring. A company founder should sit in on interviews for a while to ensure everyone hired shares the same values. Another way to test culture fit is to invite potential hires to work in the office for a period to see how they gel with the team. You can ask the team to weigh in on fit because they *are* the culture; their feedback is important.

According to a TINYpulse survey, employees' happiness depends more on how they rate coworkers than how they rate supervisors, so hiring the right teammates is doubly important. People prefer coworkers who are team players and collaborative.

Besides hiring, your culture should be built into everything you do. Use your culture to help manage your team, including it in evaluations, feedback, promotions, and bonuses. This all reiterates the importance of your core values and further reinforces your commitment to them. Use your culture as a guide in your business decisions like whom to partner with, how to spend money, and where to cut costs. Use your culture as a compass for building personality into your products. If you have a quirky personality, then you might add some quirky, hidden features to your product that will carry through to your customers.

Susan Strayer LaMotte of exaqueo believes you should turn your values into work rules, or guidelines for behavior. She explains, "Let's say you value customer service. What does that mean? Do you value empowering employees to spend time building deep customer relationships? Or are you more focused on volume-driven problem solving? It's the same skill: customer service. But by spelling out what the work rule is and what it means, you can hire the person who is good at the right kind of customer service for your business."

Care.com, a caregiver marketplace, is an example of a company that really infuses its culture into all it does. After incorporating in October 2006, Care.com set its cultural values in November. And what the owners realized was that believing in people—teamwork—is the foundation of culture.

"It is the belief in your people. It's not just lip service," says founder and CEO Sheila Marcelo. "Because if you think you're the smartest in the room, you're better than everybody else, you're the more highly educated … you're drinking your own Kool-Aid, how are you going to get anything done in the company? Building things requires a whole group of people."

When new hires inevitably ask how to succeed at Care.com, Marcelo always gives the same answer. You're already self-motivated and Type A, she says; what you should focus on is being an exceptional team player.

One of Care.com's values is being respectful, which includes a "no assholes policy." Marcelo recalls times when she actually had to take an employee out to dinner, thank the person for high performance, but explain that the person was difficult to work with and things needed to change.

> ### Sheila Marcelo
>
> Sheila Marcelo is the founder and CEO of Care.com, which helps people find caregivers for children, seniors, and pets. Founded in 2006, the company has grown to more than 9.5 million members in 16 countries and 357 full-time employees. Care.com has raised around $110 million in funding and went public in 2014. Before Care.com, Marcelo worked at tech companies, including UPromise, TheLadders.com, and Matrix Partners. Her interest in technology was sparked by time as a management consultant and teaching fellow at Harvard Business School.

Over time, Marcelo also learned that believing in people means giving them the responsibility for their own culture. When employees complained that Care.com wasn't fun enough, the management team rented a bus and surprised everyone with a day of bowling. But Marcelo realized this wasn't the key to a fun culture. So the next time someone complained about lack of fun, she told them: it's your job to make it fun. If you want to go outside and play Frisbee in the afternoon, do it—who's stopping you? Marcelo and Care.com understand that you have to translate your values into action—repeated action. Traditions take time to nurture, but they will take root in an everyday office environment where your core values are front and center.

Remember that there's a difference between core values and company perks. Culture is not about perks; it's about values. Perks can be fun, but they should be based on values. For example, unlimited vacation days would make sense only in an overall culture of trusting employees or work-life balance. Just layering on fun perks won't give you a healthy culture unless they all tie back to the master plan: your company's core values.

As your company grows, you eventually might hire or select someone whose job it is to focus on culture. After raising a round of funding in 2009, Eventbrite cofounder Julia Hartz asked, "What would happen if a founder of a company ... focused on people?" She decided to do just that—and five years later, with a team of more than 300, she still does. When your company gets to a certain point, your core job is managing the people and culture you've built.

Julia Hartz

Julia Hartz cofounded Eventbrite in 2006 with her husband Kevin Hartz and Renaud Visage. The San Francisco startup offers a platform for event organizers to sell and promote their event tickets. As of September 2013, Eventbrite had processed $2 billion in total ticket sales, had nearly 60,000 event organizers using the platform, and had more than $100 million in funding. Hartz came to Eventbrite from the television industry, working for FX and MTV Networks.

The Harsh Reality

We've glimpsed at what can happen when your company develops a bad culture, as was the case with Tony Hsieh's previous company, LinkExchange. It went so far as to cripple the motivation of the cofounders. If that's what the cofounders were feeling, you can only imagine what the rest of the company felt like. That's why it's crucial to grab the cultural bull by the horns early, laying the groundwork for cultural success.

But it's not always a smooth journey—where you have a brainstorming meeting, come up with your values, and suddenly everything is perfect. At Care.com, first-time CEO Marcelo once had to deal with an employee who posted a profane comment on a public blog post. In a Thursday meeting, she and some other executives decided that the comment went against their company values, and they fired that person. She apologized for the situation to the whole company on Friday, but she felt troubled the entire weekend. Something wasn't right; she had been too hasty. So she called the fired employee, asked the person to come back, and had to stand up in front of everyone on Monday and admit her mistake. She decided that the values of compassion and embracing failure were more important. It takes time to figure out what your culture is.

You may be tempted to hire for talent only and not culture fit, but you'll soon see the consequences. In a post called "Never Ever Compromise: Hiring for Culture Fit," serial entrepreneur Elad Gil writes, "Every single founder I know who has compromised on culture fit has regretted it due to the disruptions it has caused their company (having to fire the bad fits, creating a crappy work environment, good people quitting, trust eroding between coworkers, product moving in the wrong direction, bad actors building power bases, misaligned incentives emerging in the organization, etc.)."[1]

"One bad hire can lead to a domino effect of more bad hires and decisions costing a company millions," echoes Hsieh. That's when you have to fire someone. Sometimes it will be someone whom you don't really want to fire, but it has to be done.

---

[1] http://blog.eladgil.com/2010/06/startups-when-how-to-fire-employee-at.html

On the flip side, there are going to be times when good employees leave, and it will negatively affect your company and its culture. Only a healthy culture will be able to bounce back from these setbacks.

Celebrate: Enjoy the Journey

I love seeing how various companies get creative with the sole purpose of inspiring and motivating their teams. Here are four companies that focus on group activities, employee perks, and celebrations to motivate and create a specific culture for their brand.

- *Eventbrite,* an online events management platform, offers employees a kegerator, massages, table tennis competitions, a giant Jenga set, and an annual talent show. The company also offers Brite Camp, where employees teach classes to one another during lunch, fostering continued learning.

- *HubSpot,* an inbound marketing software company, offers new hires a way to get their questions answered with an Ask the Founders Anything session (think: transparency and communication). In addition to the office table tennis table, foosball, and standing desks, employees can sign up for a Mystery Dinner, where they get randomly matched with other employees for a dinner out. Other activities you might find employees enjoying are brewing beers, playing board games, doing yoga, playing in a house band, and teaching others everything from origami to poker to whiskey tasting.

- *SpareFoot* is a self-storage company based in Austin. Its values include a work-hard-play-hard attitude, transparency, and teamwork. During the process of onboarding new employees, the new hire has to tell the team about his or her favorite song, movie, food, and color. And in the office, there's a bar with the clock permanently set to 5 PM (hey, it's 5 o'clock somewhere). To foster continued teamwork, the company offers lunchtime classes called Eatucation and encourages team building through hosted events, such as a company prom and a boat trip to Lake Travis.

- Denver-based *TrackVia* helps businesses build applications and believes in results, doing right by customers and colleagues, thinking like a customer, taking action, taking pride in your work, creating a fun and rewarding workplace, doing what you say, and being positive (finding a solution). Employees get gym memberships, coffee from a monthly mobile barista, and tickets to Rockies baseball games. All the while, the TrackVia Action Committee dreams up new perks that tie back to the company's values.

Final Thoughts

Company culture matters. Whether you're a startup or a large organization, the people who make up your business and the culture that guides it are crucial to success. If you want to read the Bible of company culture, I recommend you check out Tony Hsieh's book *Delivering Happiness*. You'll learn a lot about Zappos and how it approaches culture, and you may even be inspired to take a field trip to sunny, downtown Las Vegas and tour Zappos's headquarters, which the company welcomes.

Can't make the trip? Check out the Zappos Insights training materials and videos (online at ZapposInsights.com). You can review the Zappos Culture Book, which is an annual snapshot of Zappos culture with input from employees (good and bad). *Delivering Happiness* even spun out as its own company to take on helping other companies with their culture.

Tony Hsieh may have explained it best when he said, "A company's culture and a company's brand are really just two sides of the same coin. The brand is just a lagging indicator of the company's culture."

What does that mean? A brand comes from all the interactions that customers have with the company, and how employees act in those interactions is influenced by the culture. If you get the culture right, you have a much better chance of having positive customer interactions. We have always believed that about Tech Cocktail—if our culture is fun, positive, and educational, then our attendees and readers will see it via our events and articles. If the culture is right, everyone wins.

10 Celebration

Celebration is an active state, an act of expressing reverence or appreciation… Celebration is a confrontation, giving attention to the transcendent meaning of one's actions.

—Abraham Joshua Heschel

The startup journey is a hard one. It's a roller coaster ride where you can't always see the track ahead, so you just hang on and ride through amazing highs and lonely lows. On the good days, you want to belt out your favorite song at the top of your lungs while driving down the highway. But on the bad days, you might not want to get out of bed. You might want to give up on your company—or even worse, give up on life. I've seen it happen to startup founders and friends.

The common advice around startups about pulling all-nighters, sucking it up, and "just f***ing doing it" doesn't acknowledge the real emotional tolls of leading a startup. Starting up a business can both charge and drain your energy simultaneously. Fortunately, in my years of running various ventures, I discovered an underutilized yet extremely important tool that can leverage big and small wins and keep you and your team focused and motivated during the not-so-good times. This tool is celebration.

Yes, that's right—I'm calling celebration a tool. In this case, celebration as a tool means recognizing accomplishments of all sizes throughout the startup journey and sharing them with your team, customers, and community. You can use celebration as a tool to help yourself, your team, and your brand. Celebration can help you through low times and get you back on solid ground.

Company

If you think about the productivity cycle, celebration is a key part of it. You ideate, create, celebrate, and start over again. If you pause for a moment to commemorate an accomplishment—making a sale, fixing a bug, or acquiring a user—you can boost morale and energy, encourage progress, and motivate employees to work toward future celebratory moments.

By celebrating accomplishments both big and small, people feel recognized. We all want recognition and reward. When I was a kid, my parents recognized my good grades by dangling them from magnets on the refrigerator. Gold stars and smiley faces worked as motivators. But now, in the hustle, founders may forget to say thank you to employees for their hard work (since founders take their own long hours for granted). Building in celebrations can be a way to say that thank you. "Entrepreneurship is every bit as much about the spirit as it is about the skills," says author Bill Aulet, the managing director of the Martin Trust Center for MIT Entrepreneurship.

Celebration can also send signals to your team. "By celebrating wins and milestones, you demonstrate confidence and a bright future. You are signaling that things are going well and good times are ahead," says Lenny Kharitonov, president of SSTL Inc.

Brand

Celebration can also help your brand by communicating your successes to the outside world. Although I come from the Midwest, where tooting your own horn is generally frowned upon, I quickly learned a lesson that I live by as an entrepreneur: if you don't tell your story, no one will. No one cares about your story more than you do. So you have to be willing to scream it from the top of a mountain.

Help yourself by communicating about company wins, partnerships, and more on your blog, at events, and to the press. Let it contribute to your marketing. I think about it more as a continued story, a dialogue of your progress. Acknowledging and celebrating your company successes helps your story get out there, garner attention from more people, and be heard by people (investors, potential hires, or partners) who might care about your company. People don't gravitate to a void. They're attracted to what they know, and hearing from you regularly helps make any dialogue easier to pick right up.

Science

I didn't just make this all up. Celebration is a type of savoring, an emotional skill that includes mindfulness, full engagement in the present, and an appreciation of what's happening now. And it's been shown to contribute to happiness and well-being. Celebrations help prevent you from being deterred by setbacks and help you see things in the best light, which is another skill called positive reframing. People who can see the positive even in negative situations score higher on tests of self-esteem, optimism, and hardiness, and the technique is particularly useful for perfectionists.

Celebrations can also help reinforce a sense of personal accomplishment, which fuels motivation. If you look at Maslow's hierarchy of needs, a theory of human motivation, part of our esteem needs are achievement and respect from others. In startups, the sense of achievement can feel rather low because it takes awhile before the company is succeeding. Celebrations along the way create little successes that help your self-esteem and positively influence motivation.

Daniel H. Pink, the *New York Times* and *Wall Street Journal* best-selling author of *Drive,* puts it well: he explains that rewards actually don't make us perform better in creative work. Instead, he says, we should cultivate intrinsic motivation. Having a sense of purpose is part of intrinsic motivation, and celebrations can help reinforce that purpose. Intrinsic rewards are the very rewards that drive us to work, to vote, to jump on the scale, and to smile at our reflection in the mirror. Feeling good feels good. Celebrating feels good and fuels the reward chain.

How to Celebrate

With all this talk about celebration as a tool, let's dive into what it actually looks like. We're not talking about popping bubbly throughout the day. That would make for an interesting work culture, but it's not really healthy or sustainable. Let's start by examining some instances of what you might celebrate and how.

As a startup you may hit goals or milestones, launch your product, get funded, start making money, sign a partnership deal, win an award, get press, have individual daily or weekly achievements, grow your team, or make it through a big week in one piece. Each achievement calls for a celebration, probably of different magnitude.

Internal Celebrations

The team at a startup called inqiri does something called Whiskey Wednesdays, where they go to a local Irish pub together. James Elste, chief executive officer (CEO) of inqiri, explains, "It involves the acknowledgment of the progress we are making and successes we are celebrating, whether it is a minor achievement or major milestone." He goes on: "I think it's important to celebrate success frequently in a startup environment. It … keeps people motivated and builds an esprit de corps throughout the team."

Chicago-based BrightTag, a tag management system for publishers and website owners, uses celebrations to showcase development progress. After each build, the development team bakes a cake, and the entire company gets together and celebrates the new code push. This gives the development team recognition from the rest of the BrightTag team with a positive, tasty reinforcement of the progress they're making.

With the mission to create products that help people live healthier lives, New York–based Noom celebrates the growth of its team. Every time Noom has to expand its office to fit more people, a celebration is held on Friday evening. The first time this was done, the employees actually broke down a wall with a sledgehammer. Another time, everyone ate lobster rolls. Creativity is key: you don't have to celebrate the same way every time. (From a safety perspective, I'm glad Noom didn't up its game by going in next with a wrecking ball, then a bulldozer, and so on.)

Bulu Box, a Lincoln, Nebraska–based monthly subscription service of vitamin, supplement, health, and weight loss products, uses celebration regularly by hosting everything from bowling night to a breakfast of cinnamon rolls and mimosas. "Anything that rallies us together, even for a little while, to recognize how far we've come," say cofounders Paul and Stephanie Jarrett.

External Celebrations

Externally you can also use celebration as a tool to connect with the community, press, investors, potential new employees, and more.

Lauren Thorp (the wife of our VP of Marketing and Community Development, Justin Thorp) was working full-time in finance while creating Umba. Umba started as a monthly subscription service so that handmade goods lovers like herself could easily discover great items while learning about the designers who made the products.

Taking Justin's advice, Thorp reluctantly pitched Umba at a local tech meetup in Washington, DC. And the response was a wake-up call for her. The interest and support from the community made her realize that her passion-fueled side project really had potential. Not only that, but investor Paul Singh was in the audience and invited her to the 500 Startups accelerator that summer. Without taking a moment to externally pause, share, and celebrate, she may have never gotten the attention of an investor

Paul Singh

Paul Singh is a former partner at the 500 Startups accelerator and founder of Disruption Corporation, which offers tools, research, and advice to startups and investors. Disruption Corporation includes the Crystal Tech Fund, a fund for post-seed startups; Indicate.io, which allows investors to research startups and track their portfolios; and Dashboard.io, which allows founders to compare their metrics to their peers', based in Crystal City, Arlington, Virginia, an urban neighborhood overlooking Washington, DC and National Airport. Indicate.io tracks more than 65,000 startups and more than 70 portfolios. Singh was a serial entrepreneur and did consulting through a company he called Results Junkies.

and moved her passion project to a full-time job, catapulting her into her startup journey.

Uber, the mobile marketplace for on-demand transportation, has done an extraordinary job using celebration as a tool to unify its communities. For example, on Valentine's Day, Uber drivers delivered roses to customers. Right before Christmas, the drivers delivered Christmas trees, specifically ordered from their site in certain markets. The company has also done similar promotions with ice cream on those hot summer days; burrito deliveries down in Austin, Texas; and even kittens!

What these celebratory moments do is create joy for their growing communities—and in doing so, Uber is creating allies. When Uber launches in new cities, it's not always warmly welcomed from local officials. In fact, some cities have long-standing, rigid laws in place to regulate the transportation industry. Some of these laws block Uber from operating—the company has received a few cease-and-desist orders. And instead of fighting them alone or giving up, Uber looks to its loyal community of allies. The allies sign petitions and speak out against the officials who are trying to shut Uber out. Call this brilliant strategy, marketing, or whatever you will, but leveraging the tool of celebration publicly to unite its community to fight for the right to Uber has been quite effective. Including customers or partners in your celebrations is key to building relationships and affinity.

Tech Cocktail uses celebration as the fabric of what we do as a news and events company. Our mission is to help entrepreneurs enjoy the startup life journey by providing resources, connections, and community. How do we do it? *We shine a light on and celebrate the accomplishments of startup communities.* We leverage celebratory moments to bring together thousands of entrepreneurs, startup founders, developers, designers, investors, and media at hundreds of events through the years. We also share those accomplishments through our online media coverage so other communities around the world can see what each market is achieving.

In a model similar to the TV show *American Idol,* Tech Cocktail tours the country to host events in various cities, rallying together the community and offering startups a chance to showcase their products. Startups can participate in their local pitch event, and the community votes on the best startup. The local winners are further narrowed down by a group of judges, with the best ones advancing to our national startup competition and conference called Tech Cocktail Celebrate. At that point, community support is behind the winners as they represent various regions at the finals, with a chance at national exposure to media and investors—not to mention bragging rights with the rest of the country.

Personal Celebration

Celebration can help you personally, too. As you achieve different milestones, you can have little celebrations for yourself and even for your family and friends, who support your startup journey.

Tom Nardone is the president of PriveCo, a company based in Troy, Michigan, that helps keep your purchases private. When a sale is made, Nardone sometimes shares this with his eight-year-old son. "He likes to hear about the business and he smiles when it goes well," explains Nardone.

Detroit-based Savorfull founder Stacy Goldberg celebrates by traveling. "I take myself out of my office setting and work from a beautiful location to both reward myself and foster creativity!" she says.

I give myself breaks, too. Whether it be a walk outside or a chance to catch up on movies I haven't seen, I celebrate little daily milestones. The larger personal milestones are celebrated with special dinners or travel. After our first year running Tech Cocktail full-time, Jen and I celebrated our survival and licked our wounds by taking a two-week workation in Kauai. We would get up early every day to watch the sunrise, eat breakfast, and then work until about noon or a little afterward. After 5 or 6 hours of work, we would hit the road for some Kauai adventures, including hiking and exploring beaches. It was a celebration that was good for our mental and physical health and well-being. We came back to take on the new year with just as much vigor and intensity as the year before.

Moments of Celebration

Celebratory moments don't have to be huge. High fives, Friday afternoon drinks, lunch or dinner out, a break to chat with your team about nonwork stuff, or a walk all count. As a fun example, Chicago-based WeDeliver celebrates by making things together, from bow ties to hot sauce called AwesomeSauce.

Entrepreneur and consultant Tony Rappa once struggled for 3 hours to edit a video, then finally got it and decided to treat himself to a donut and coffee. "I sat in my car for a few minutes enjoying my treat and thinking about the fact that I hadn't given up on my task. I actually spent time thinking about what this little triumph could mean in the overall journey. I realized that it's these little moments, these little wins that will define how I handle myself in the next challenge and ultimately my level of success."

As a company, consider creating systems to make celebration systematic. This will ensure it's not just random, but built into the culture and tied back to your core values.

RevTrax, a promotional platform for online-to-offline sales using digital coupons and offers, has a committee of employees called Fun-Trax. They plan team events such as happy hours, lunches, and sporting events. Jonathan Treiber, cofounder and CEO, says, "We have a fantastic group of smart, dedicated employees, so we like to celebrate RevTrax's success by rewarding the team for the hard work they put in day in and day out."

Famigo, an Austin-based company helping developers and the next generation of educators reach families, has a Mandatory Fun Day on the last Friday of every month. The team bonds over activities that include laser tag, wakeboarding, and barbecues. "We find it more important to celebrate the little victories on a regular basis and get everybody out of the office regularly," says Q Beck, cofounder and CEO.

Celebrate in Moderation

Celebration is a great tool, but like any tool it can be used too much or the wrong way. When this happens, moments of celebration aren't special anymore, so they don't have the desired effect of motivation and team building. Excessive celebration can detract from working time—not to mention, it can be bad for your startup's reputation. Too much partying and drinking is not the reputation you want out on the streets—and especially not what you want reaching investors or press.

There has already been some criticism of the tech scene for this. For example, *Start-Ups: Silicon Valley*, a reality show following entrepreneurs in the Valley, was criticized for portraying too much drinking and partying and not enough working. The same thing was said about *The Social Network* movie.

In the *Washington Post* article "Tech Community: Are We MTV or TED?" Francisco Dao explains that, "Anyone who spends more than a week making the rounds of tech industry parties in San Francisco will quickly notice a whole group of people who seem far more concerned with 'making the scene' than they are with actual entrepreneurship."

You might call excessive celebration self-congratulation. Here's how to avoid being self-congratulatory:

- *Size:* Celebration is in proportion to the accomplishment; self-congratulation is excessive.
- *Purpose:* Celebration is meant to recognize past work and motivate future work; self-congratulation is simply to reflect on how awesome you are and how much you're crushing it.

- *Venue:* Celebration can be private or public; self-congratulation often has a deliberately public aspect meant to impress others or brag.

Final Thoughts

Celebration is a tool. It can be used internally and externally to keep your outlook positive through the ups and downs of your startup journey, motivate your team, and also connect you with your community. As a company, you need to determine how much is too much. You don't want to rely on celebrations for everything, but it can be that secret sauce that gets you over various humps and keeps you and your team motivated. Your culture, led by your core values, can be a guide to keep your celebrations in balance and tied back to your overall goals. So use this tool for good, and let the celebrations begin!

11 Relationships

In my experience, there is no such thing as luck.

—Obi-Wan Kenobi

Attending a tech conference in Paris, Laura Fitton (known to many as @pistachio on Twitter) desperately wanted to meet Doc Searls, the blogger and coauthor of *The Cluetrain Manifesto*. But Fitton knew a thing or two about relationships—namely, rushing up to him after his talk wasn't the right approach.

So Fitton was patient. She started by chatting with Searls's wife. A few times during the conference, she made eye contact with him. And finally, she approached Searls after his talk and said humbly, "I hope I haven't crossed into the borderline of being rude, because I know I've seen you and we've been at events together a bunch of times and we've made eye contact, but I really don't like approaching people who are in demand as much as you are because I feel like I'm just adding to that weight."

To her delight, Searls didn't find her rude. In fact, he grabbed his coauthor David Weinberger and they all spent the night dining and hanging out—and have been great friends since. Fitton asks, "Had I bum-rushed him the first three times we were in the same room, would I have gotten that much trust and kindness and openness to just explore and see where it goes?"

She likens this to the story of the fox in *The Little Prince*. The fox tells the Little Prince he can't just hang out with him, he has to tame him first. So he advises the Little Prince to come every day and sit nearby but not to try to play with him yet. Developing patience is the lesson here, and something we can all take away. So many people need to cultivate more patience when meeting new people. It's an exchange, a conversation, not a one-way opportunity to talk at someone.

Fitton credits her relationship-building skills with helping her transition from a completely unknown, isolated mom of two kids to someone who was quoted in a Seth Godin book, convinced Guy Kawasaki that Twitter was interesting, wrote her own book, became the chief executive officer (CEO) of a venture-funded company called OneForty, and sold to HubSpot.

Social Media

When I was blogging on *Somewhat Frank,* it was the relationships that I cultivated across the tight-knit blogosphere that made it so important to my everyday routine. I met fellow blog-gers Michael Arrington, who had just started TechCrunch; Richard MacManus, who had been writing *ReadWriteWeb;* Pete Cashmore, who started a site for the latest trends, the future, and fast news for early adopters called Mashable; and Brian Solis, who was creating his own personal brand at PR2.0, which eventually turned into Bri-anSolis.com. We all met each other and started linking to and commenting on one another's blogs. I didn't know these people would turn into industry leaders in the tech and startup space; we just shared a common interest and enjoyed exchanging ideas.

Brian Solis

Brian Solis was another early Web pioneer, specializing in social media. In 2011, he joined as a principal at Altimeter Group, a research and advi-sory firm that helps compa-nies with disruption. Solis is the author of several books, includ-ing *The End of Business as Usual, Engage,* and *What's the Future of Business?* He speaks frequently about social media, disruptive technology, and the consumer landscape. Based in San Fran-cisco, Solis is also the host and curator of the Pivot Conference on new media.

By 2006, my blog was growing, I was traveling more for my blogging efforts, and I started to guest write on TechCrunch. Having met Arrington in 2005, I reached out to give him a hand on writing some longer-format indus-try comparison pieces on topics such as RSS feed readers, maps, and music. They were the most popular posts on TechCrunch in 2006, and startup founders, investors, entrepreneurs, and companies were using my research and articles for research and development (R&D). And they opened up relationships to readers who appreciated my insights and perspective and sent me feedback by e-mail. For example, Dick Costolo, then-CEO of FeedBurner, wrote, "Very cool guest post in TechCrunch. That was awesome." It was simple e-mail messages like this that kept me going with my daily routine and clawing to get out of my day job, looking to jump to freedom. Little did I know that just

Evan Williams

Evan Williams was CEO of Twitter from 2008 to 2010 and is credited as the inventor of the term *blogger*. He is the cofounder of Pyra Labs (which created Blogger, acquired by Google), Twitter, and the Obvious Corporation (which created Medium). Medium is a publishing platform designed to make it easy to share ideas and enable ideas from anywhere to be heard. Medium raised $25 million in January 2014. Williams is based in San Francisco.

four years later, Costolo would take over for Evan Williams as the CEO of Twitter and would lead them to a successful initial public offering (IPO). You never know where people are going to end up.

Every person you meet or interact with could be the next great entrepreneur, big supporter, long-term customer, investor, or maybe a friend. You never know. Although this may seem like common sense, some of us simply don't put relationship building into practice. Putting it into practice means treating everyone with respect and giving them your full attention and interest if you happen to be chatting with them.

The most important lesson I've learned over the years regarding building relationships may seem pretty trivial, yet it is very powerful:

People care about themselves and the things they care about.

It's inspired by Dale Carnegie's granddaddy of all relationship management books, *How to Win Friends & Influence People* (first published in 1937). I have managed my relationships from that premise for years, and it has been extremely helpful. I've even given it to friends and relatives.

Rather than looking for people who can help you, why not look for ways to help the people you want to connect with? It's much more likely to create a lasting relationship, and it feels a lot better, too. If you start by helping people—both those you want to meet and those you don't—good things will happen. You'll be racking up karma points while also meeting new people. It's the best way to grow your network of relationships. Some of those relationships will turn into lasting connections and friendships.

How Relationships Can Help You

Relationships are often neglected by entrepreneurs because *networking* has a bad reputation. But Priceline's former chief technology officer (CTO) Scott Case believes that founders of successful companies tend to have a strong network and use it to solve problems, such as finding funding, engineers, partnerships, and distribution. This is exactly why relationships matter—you can make yourself, your company, and your life based on the people with whom you have relationships. He says, "Founders tend to spend an enormous amount of time doing product development ... The thing that I see as I travel across the country over and over again is a lack of network development—a lack of founders building a community around their idea at the very beginning."

The expression "luck surface area" was coined by Jason Roberts, a serial entrepreneur and cohost of the podcast TechZing. He believes luck surface area or serendipity "is directly proportional to the degree to which you do something you're passionate about combined with the total number of people to whom this is effectively communicated." So in his mind, luck is equated with *doing*

Scott Case

Scott Case was the cofounding CTO of Priceline, the name-your-own-price travel-booking site. Recently, he was CEO of the Startup America Partnership, which supported startups to help create jobs and fuel the American economy. In 2013, Startup America partnered with Startup Weekend to launch UP Global, a network that connects entrepreneurs with communities and resources. Based in DC, Case is now a board member of UP Global and launched his own venture: Main Street Genome, which builds software to model the main street economy. Case has also worked with nonprofits such as Malaria No More and Network for Good.

multiplied by *telling*. If you increase your luck surface area, you are increasing your odds that your story will get out, thus offering more potential opportunities.

Zvi Band is a Washington, DC–based founder who now believes in Roberts' luck surface area—although that wasn't always the case. Band is a developer and, like many developers, is an admittedly introverted guy. A few years ago, he thought networking was, in his own words, "total f***ing bullshit."

Band was working at a consulting firm and eventually became interested in startups. He soon realized that he needed to meet others who knew more about startups than he did. So out he went and started to meet people at different local events.

As he continued to get out and attend events, Band's network grew bigger and bigger. Band attributes much of his consulting and startup success to his network. "Not only did I have myself looking out for my venture, I had other people looking out for me, too," he says. Thanks to them and their word-of-mouth publicity, he was able to run a successful consultancy for four years without much pitching or marketing.

But he also knew he was not great at managing his relationships. So his life came full circle when he, an introverted developer who had seen no value in networks or meeting people, decided to build a startup focused on helping people manage their relationships. He threw together a prototype that scratched his own itch and solved a problem. This prototype turned into a startup called Contactually, a platform that helps you keep track of all your contacts with ease. When Contactually was first funded, 13 of 15 investors came from Band's network.

Besides introducing you to customers and investors, relationships can help you in a number of other ways, not least of which is emotional support. Starting up is really hard work, and it helps to have people who know what you're going through. If your network includes seasoned startup founders, you can turn to them on those days when you feel like you're running out of steam. They can help you brainstorm solutions to overcome your problems.

If you cultivate relationships with developers, designers, and others, you may end up hiring them someday. I keep a secret wish list of potential hires, adding new people as I meet them and removing people when they no longer fit anymore. (Bo Fishback of Zaarly one-ups me: he makes his own list and then asks all his new hires for *their* lists!)

One person on my list was Justin Thorp, a DC-based developer who had moved into community management and marketing for AddThis and then HelloWallet. Justin is probably one of the most approachable people I've met, and he loved Tech Cocktail. He was at our early Tech Cocktail events in DC and even flew to Chicago to attend our first conference. I always thought he would be great to have on our team to help build our community, as well as the direction of our news products. Five years later, I had an opportunity to hire Justin, and he did not disappoint. He has led the growth of Tech Cocktail's event and editorial footprint while also helping to build new processes within the organization as we formalize from a bootstrapped company to a funded startup fueled for growth.

Lesson learned: make note of the people you meet, and maybe someday you'll hire them or help them get hired elsewhere. They might be the next people who invest in you to help you live the dream. They could also include a budding journalist at a local publication, who just a few years down the road takes over at a major national publication. *You never know where people will end up.*

Tips for Relationship Building

So you want to improve your odds at creating lasting relationships? Figure out what relationships you're looking for: mentors and advisors, entrepreneurial peers, investors, general industry relationships—you can actively decide.

If you don't know anyone, start attending local events or meetups. Speaker-style events such as our Sessions series showcase thought leaders who might be good mentors, and you may meet interesting peers. Think of creative ways to introduce yourself at the event or online and see if these leaders will meet you for a 15-minute coffee. In that initial meeting, don't unload all your problems. Ask questions, and let them do more of the talking as you get to know each other. Afterward, just keep in contact. Once you have the communication lines open, it becomes easier to ask for advice or introductions.

If you're too shy or introverted to go out and meet people, you may want to consider teaming up with someone else. Pair up with someone in your network—ideally someone who can sustain a conversation. That person can fill in any awkward pauses and help lead the conversation forward.

When trying to expand your network, hands down, warm introductions go a lot further than reaching out on your own. By *warm introductions,* I mean an introduction to someone through a mutual contact. Fitton recommends starting with the people closest to you and asking them who they know who can help you—she did that with One-Forty. Fitton's friends didn't know any angel investors but kept making introductions for her, and eventually she connected with the right people.

She explains, "Start with the people who already know you, love you, and believe in you … because those are your strongest advocates." Or better yet, do the work for them—do your research. Visit their LinkedIn or AngelList profile and

---

AngelList

AngelList was founded in 2010 by Naval Ravikant and Babak Nivi, who had worked together on a startup advice site called Venture Hacks. AngelList is a platform that connects people within the startup community: entrepreneurs can meet investors, potential employees, and one another. It recently launched Syndicates, where accredited investors can raise a fund with other investors who agree to invest in any startups the first investor chooses. Angel List is based in San Francisco.

see whom they've invested in or whom they're connected with that you might like to meet.

For a list of tools for cultivating and managing relationships, check out http://tech.co/book.

Relationships for the Long Term

Once you've met new people, it's important to maintain those relationships. This will take time and follow-up on your part. Building relationships requires repeated contact, online and offline. Try sending your new contacts an interesting article, making an introduction, recommending an event for them to attend, or telling them about a competitor. You can also take the opportunity to share some updates about yourself, without bragging.

"It's through those interactions of being able to understand the person well, feeling comfortable helping them out, and then them feeling comfortable receiving that help, where we can truly develop these bonds," says Andy White, a partner at the Downtown Project's VegasTechFund.

Make this part of your daily routine. Brittany Hodak, cofounder of ZinePak, spends 90 minutes on Monday mornings scanning LinkedIn and other sites for job changes and promotions and sends congratulations and invitations to lunch or coffee. Band has it down to a science and recommends keeping in touch with potential investors and hires

> ### Downtown Project
> Led by Tony Hsieh, the Downtown Project is a $350 million revitalization project in downtown Las Vegas. It divides its funds in a few key areas: $50 million for investing in small businesses, $50 million for tech startups, $50 million for education, and $200 million for real estate. The goals of the Downtown Project include creating a downtown that lets you live, work, and play all within walking distance; creating the most community-focused large city; and creating the coworking and colearning capital of the world.

every 7 days, sales leads every 10 days, top users and current investors every 15 days, and partners, advisors, future investors, and other entrepreneurs every 30 days.

The Harsh Reality

Building, maintaining, and managing relationships is a full-time job. There are a variety of personalities out there, and some people are just not nice. Even if you're trying to help them, they may be rude or difficult to deal with. You can get rejected. You remember that girl or guy you asked out on a date who said no? It happens here as well. Trust me, there have been people who haven't given me the time of day, but I don't give up easily.

Building and managing relationships can be even more difficult if you're introverted. "I do like people generally, but the activity and the effort is just painful ... I just don't like all the rigamarole that goes around these introductions at large events," says Micah Baldwin, founder and CEO of Graphicly. "At the end of going to something, I'll be exhausted."

And you'll probably stumble along the way. "Early in my career, I often rushed into the business side of things way too early, without really getting to know who I was speaking to. This sometimes led to miscommunication and a conflict of interest," says Jonathan Birch, an online development consultant at Mediaworks. You don't want to be known as someone who is only out for yourself.

You're also likely to run into people who take advantage of you. Not everyone out there has pure intentions. People lie, cheat, and hustle. You may meet some of these people and even do business with them. I know we have, and it stinks. A few years ago we were working with a company at one of our events and they insisted—very loudly—that we had wronged them, actually bullying one of our team members. We had an e-mail chain a mile long that indicated we had not and that they were actually trying to take advantage of us, but nothing we said was going to change their mind. When they tried to cause a public scene at an event, we simply asked them to leave, looking to defuse the situation and follow up with them afterward. Just know that as you build relationships, you can't control everything or everyone. As I tell my team, act with integrity, take the high road, and move on. Next.

Celebrate: Enjoy the Journey

Your attitude toward relationships will directly affect how much fun you have while growing your network. If you can be genuinely interested in people and embrace the idea of getting to know others, then it will be more enjoyable—regardless of whether it yields benefits to your business. "I no longer ask people what they do for a living—that's lame. Instead, I ask them what they're passionate about," explains Tony Rappa, an entrepreneur and consultant. He says that's been a game changer for building solid relationships.

Micah Baldwin reflects on his relationships by saying, "I don't really consider myself having a network—I just have a bunch of friends. I think that's the key. I've never tried to network in my life. I've only tried to meet interesting people and to be friendly. I don't ever think about what I can get. I think about only what I can give." Baldwin knows the importance of helping others first.

Relationships are what will energize you and fuel you, making life worthwhile. They take time to develop and nurture. Look at building relationships as making friends, not just networking. Friends are the kind of allies you want on your side.

Final Thoughts

Remember, people care about themselves and what they believe in. Think of what others care about from their perspective, not yours; this will ensure you make more friends and make stronger connections.

It can feel like an odd balance—you want to build relationships and just see where they lead, but eventually you might need to ask for something and take opportunities when they're presented to you. Carpe diem. Learning to ask for what you want is an art. "Ninety-five percent of the time we don't get what we want, we never ask," says Fitton. "You cheat the heck out of yourself when you're too afraid to pursue an opportunity... So what if someone turns you down." As Wayne Gretzky says, "You miss 100 percent of the shots you don't take."

Part 4
Sales and Marketing

12 Marketing

Give them quality. That's the best kind of advertising.

—Milton Hershey

On a sunny, spring day in Washington, DC, the farm-to-table salads and wrap upstart called Sweetgreen was struggling to get its second location off the ground. The storefront was the only thing on that particular side of the street—and now there weren't enough customers.

While Nathaniel Ru manned the store, his cofounders, Jonathan Neman and Nicolas Jammet, decided to try something to stir up excitement and make a musical scene. They aimed a newly purchased black speaker toward Dupont Circle and set up a brown folding table on the sidewalk. With these amateur DJs just outside the restaurant and free samples available, people crossed the street and stopped by. The founders had created demand for Sweetgreen.

When the sidewalk party grew too large, they moved the gathering to the parking lot behind the store. They brought in a stage and got local bands to play, attracting 500 attendees. The Sweetlife Festival, a party with a purpose, was born. The street fest was all in the name of the sweet life, a core value that Sweetgreen lived by, but the music festival was also a way to market and attract new customers to its new location.

The next year Sweetgreen connected with Seth Hurwitz, one of the owners of the famous DC music venue the 9:30 Club. The founders wanted to make the Sweetlife Festival bigger, thinking 2,000 attendees would suffice. Hurwitz suggested they go all in on the Sweetlife Festival by moving it to a bigger venue and getting some bigger musical acts. The Sweetgreen team loved the band the Strokes, so they decided that if they could get the Strokes to play at Sweetlife, they would take the leap. As luck would have it, the Strokes were available and the Sweetgreen team agreed to move the Sweetlife Festival to Merriweather Post Pavilion. In its second year, 2011, the festival attracted 13,000 people and has been growing each year since.

Marketing, by definition, is a form of communication designed to acquire and retain customers while demonstrating the value of your product. The sweet life is the essence of Sweetgreen's product—delicious and healthy food—and a fun outdoor musical experience fit right into that. The Sweetlife Festival became a kind of marketing tool that attracted new customers and created delight, one of the most elusive but powerful aspects of marketing.

How did the Sweetgreen team do it? They found their tribe: a niche of customers who enjoyed their quinoa, kale, coconut water, and other fresh and healthy offerings. Then, they let their tribe tell other people, who went on to tell others, about the food experience. Music was the hook. According to Neman, "Music takes you back to another time and provides a great emotional connection."

Marketing Strategy

Coming up with your marketing strategy is an exercise in truly understanding your business. Here are some aspects to think about, before we dive into different types of marketing.

- *Customers:* To create marketing delight, understanding your customer base is crucial. Who are your customers? What do your customers want and value? What are their needs? Where do they hang out online or offline?

- *Vision:* What is your vision or *why*? That's what customers latch onto. "People don't buy what you do; they buy why you do it," says Simon Sinek, author of *Start with Why*, in a TEDx talk. Your marketing messages and communications should begin with that purpose and only then explain the how and what of your product. Sweetgreen's marketing essentially said: Do you want to enjoy the sweet life? *(why)* We have a fun and meaningful experience for you *(how)*. Come check out our music festival or our tasty food *(what)*. Sinek goes on to say, "The goal is not just to sell to people who need what you have ... the goal is to do business with people who believe what you believe"—your tribe.

  Sinek explains that these people—the innovators and early adopters, consisting of about 16 percent of your market—are most influenced by their limbic brains, where trust and loyalty are cultivated. You reach that part of the brain with your *why* message. Only after they're on board will the 84 percent majority of the population be willing to give you a shot.

The final insight Sinek shares is the reason consumers follow a *why* message: to prove something about themselves. For example, Apple users buy all sorts of gadgets to demonstrate how forward thinking they are. And who do you think drives a safety-conscious Volvo? An aspiring young musician or a middle-aged college professor? "We follow those who lead not for them, but for ourselves," Sinek says.

Rachel Sklar

A former lawyer, Rachel Sklar is now a social entrepreneur, thought leader, and startup advisor. She's the cofounder of Change the Ratio, whose goal is to increase visibility and opportunity for women, and TheLi.st, which extends Change the Ratio's mission with a community platform and events. Sklar was a founding editor at the *Huffington Post,* and she continues to write about media, politics, culture, and technology. She's also a comedian, and her #CTRComedy helped get more women performing comedy at SXSW.

A great example of this is Rachel Sklar, who has spent the past few years heading up initiatives to help women be more successful. Her organization, Change the Ratio, started with the mission to increase visibility, access, and opportunity for women and other minorities. It inspired a startup called TheLi.st, which is a community platform for women: it includes a membership network, written content, and events. Whatever Sklar is doing, she has a strong following of supporters, because they believe in her vision for the world.

- *Story:* Once you know your vision, the next step is to start crafting a story around it. It's surprising to me how many entrepreneurs and startup founders are unable to articulate their story effectively. Yet startups are full of potential stories: for example, how the product weaves into customers' lives or the personal inspiration for creating it. Marketing icon and author Seth Godin believes that great stories are authentic, bold, trustworthy, and subtle; hit you at first impression; appeal to the senses; are aimed at a niche (not the masses); and agree with the customers' worldview.

TaskRabbit's founding story stems from a personal experience that many of us can sympathize with. One night, founder Leah Busque and her husband were all set to go out to dinner when they realized that they were out of dog food for their 100-pound yellow Lab, Kobe. Shouldn't it be possible to find someone nearby to pick up and deliver the food, they thought? TaskRabbit, a site for outsourcing small jobs to your neighbors, was born—and Kobe's story lives on in their marketing.

> **Leah Busque**
>
> Leah Busque founded Task-Rabbit in 2008, originally calling it RunMyErrand. The site lets you post a task that you want done, and then connect with a TaskRabbit to complete it for you. TaskRabbits are certified by the company through a background check and interview process. Based in San Francisco, TaskRabbit has raised almost $40 million in funding and has expanded to about 20 cities. Before Task-Rabbit, Busque spent seven years as a software engineer at IBM.

- *Differentiation:* Whatever your story may be, it should include a differentiator or positioning statement. This will make clear exactly how you're better than the competition. Geoffrey Moore's book *Crossing the Chasm* goes into detail on how to produce a positioning statement. It's a helpful tool and forces you to get to the heart of your value. Here is Moore's template:

> For [target customers] who are dissatisfied with [market alternative], our product is [new category] that provides [cite the breakthrough capability]. Unlike [product alternative], we have assembled [key points of competitive differentiation].

Types of Marketing

Now it's time to put all these concepts into practice, and every marketing strategy is different. You may want to use all the types of marketing
mentioned here or only a few of them; either way, it's helpful to understand your options.

Pounding the Pavement

When you're first starting up, you'll likely need to rely on your relationships to get your company off the ground. We just talked about
relationships in the previous chapter, and all those will come into play as
you reach out to your allies via e-mail, LinkedIn, Facebook, the phone,
or even in person to scramble for your first few hundred users.

Content Marketing

Content marketing includes producing blog posts, e-books, webinars,
videos, and infographics. It's using content you create to pull people
into your website and hopefully convince them to stay and use your
product.

To start, Renee Warren of Onboardly suggests that you brainstorm
the core keywords related to your business, then come up with a list of
10 topics to write around each of them. I look at it a little less scien-
tifically: just use your content to become part of a larger conversation
in your industry and provide value to your audience in an authentic,
nonpromotional way. Guest writing on another blog that your target
audience reads can be a great platform to do this. For example, Tech
Cocktail offers an easy way to sign up for an account and become
a contributor. We get lots of submissions from founders looking to
share their expertise and (in the process) get their company name
out there.

Social Media

Cultivating relationships via social media is one of the most powerful ways to market your business. The variety of social media tools available allow you to connect on new levels with your customers. Why would you want to? Because relationships can be your competitive advantage. Leverage appropriate social channels to be genuine and reveal a little more about your company, your brand, and yourself.

Amy Jo Martin is the founder of Digital Royalty, a social media consultancy and education platform. She was one of the early adopters of social media, working with people and brands that included Shaquille O'Neal, DoubleTree, and The Rock. In her book *Renegades Write the Rules,* she says, "We all want to be seen and heard by others. We want to be valued for what we can offer others. We all want to belong to a community of others who value what we value—who are, in some important way, like us. What happens when a brand fulfills these wants? People stick around for more." Without that intangible, you're simply competing on performance—and if your performance slips, your users may look elsewhere because they don't feel real loyalty.

> **Amy Jo Martin**
>
> A Twitter pioneer, Amy Jo Martin is the one who helped Shaquille O'Neal build up his personal brand on Twitter. She met him while working as director of digital media and research at the Phoenix Suns basketball team. After two years there, she grew tired of the constraints and rules and set off on her own, founding a social media consultancy called Digital Royalty. O'Neal was her first client, and she went on to work with The Rock, DoubleTree, FOX Sports, and many others. Digital Royalty is now based in Las Vegas and funded by Tony Hsieh's Downtown Project and began offering social media education programs through its Digital Royalty University in 2012. Martin is also the author of the book *Renegades Write the Rules.*

Social media can also be used to build relationships with influencers and potential new customers. AddThis community manager Ifdy Perez follows hashtags on relevant topics and contributes to the conversation when it makes sense. In some tech startup markets, hashtags are a great way to keep track of the pulse of the city. For example, in Washington, DC, you can track the #dctech hashtag; in Las Vegas, #vegastech; in Chicago, #chitech; and in Miami, #miamitech.

Pay-per-Click Advertising

Pay-per-click might mean using Google or Facebook ads to drive traffic to your landing pages or website. Google lets you target by keywords searched, and Facebook lets you target certain demographics. You'll want to go into this with a set budget and then measure click-through rates and conversion rates to see if it's worth the money.

Lead Generation

Lead generation, or lead gen for short, involves finding potential customers who show some interest in your product—essentially, building a list of e-mail addresses (or phone numbers) so you can follow up with them. To build your list of leads, you need to ask them to perform various actions that demonstrate their interest: signing up for an e-mail list, answering questions, downloading something, attending an event, or talking with someone on your team. All these activities are lead-generating activities.

To collect leads online, you can create a free offer and ask for something in return. For example, you could give away an e-book in exchange for an e-mail address. With your lead gen process, be sure to keep your customers in mind—you want to be attracting the right people. Whatever you're offering should be appealing to your target customers; otherwise, none of your leads will pan out.

E-mail Marketing

E-mail marketing can be quite effective, so it's valuable to have a list of addresses you can use. For example, once you are collecting addresses (your leads), think about the different points of contact in the customer's journey. Perhaps it's to get them in the door, or when they've just signed up for your product, abandoned a shopping cart filled with items before buying them, or purchased something.

Strike a balance between sending too many e-mail updates and fading from the recipient's memory. If you don't, you'll know—thanks to all the unsubscribes you're getting. We've all done it: signed up, received way too many updates, and then unsubscribed. Don't drive your users away.

Elizabeth Yin is the cofounder of LaunchBit, a company that focuses on helping software-as-a-service companies acquire new customers. She thinks that weekly e-mails strike that balance between too many and too few. For open rates—that is, how many e-mails actually get opened—she recommends shooting for more than 20 percent. Your e-mail software should show you those metrics.

Based in Cambridge, Massachusetts, HubSpot offers a set of software tools for inbound marketing. HubSpot's tip is to make sure your e-mails add value, rather than just promoting your product. But equally important, e-mails should have a clear call to action, the action you want the recipient to take. Then, track the click-through rate and conversion rate (how many people took some action that you asked them to take) so you know whether the campaign was successful.

SEO and SEM

Web search is another way that new customers can find out about your services. Search engine optimization (SEO) and search engine marketing (SEM) can help increase your visibility in search engines. Learning SEO and SEM can be time-consuming, so you might want to find some experts to help you.

If you understand some of the basics, such as optimizing your website or on-page SEO, your site will get more traffic. One place to start is to figure out the search keywords that you want to rank highly for: choose keywords that aren't so competitive, because it's hard to beat established players on common keywords.

Here's a quick list of other items to be thinking about as you optimize your website for SEO:

- Make page titles short and readable, and put keywords up front. Also use keywords in headings.

- Include metadata, the description of a page that shows up in search results.

- Include links to other content.

- When adding images, put keywords in the file name (rather than Image01.jpg). Don't use too many images, because it could slow down your page and decrease your search ranking.

- Produce content regularly so Google crawls your site more often.

- Put keywords in your URLs.

One crucial factor in SEO that's hard to control is how many pages link to your website. Guest posting on other sites that offer a byline and a link back can give you a big boost. Keep in mind, however, that Google and other search engines are always changing their algorithms. Something that works today may not work tomorrow.

Word of Mouth

With all your marketing initiatives, the big, ambitious goal should be to cultivate word of mouth. As Sweetgreen learned, if what you're doing makes people tell others about it, you'll spend less on marketing and quickly become known by more and more customers. This may be the most valuable way to market your product.

You can achieve word of mouth when the whole experience around your product delights, enchants, and surprises consumers. Basecamp doesn't have a marketing department or even a marketing person, and cofounder Jason Fried says marketing is everyone's job: "Bad software is bad marketing. Bad customer service is bad marketing."

Having personality can boost word of mouth. In *Personality Not Included,* a book based on his experience with hundreds of brands, author Rohit Bhargava writes, "Personality is the key element of your brand and what it stands for, and the story that your products tell to your customers. Every element of your business, from your interactions with your customers to the packaging of your product, is an element of your brand personality, and these are the elements that inspire delight or indifference."

Brian Solis, author of *What's the Future of Business?,* believes word of mouth is increasingly important as customers consult multiple sources before buying something, and recommendations from friends weigh heavily. He echoes Bhargava, saying that every touchpoint with customers—from responding to critiques to the moment they "open the box"—is an opportunity to create a brand advocate.

If you can't get organic word of mouth, you can create different incentives within your product or service to encourage it by rewarding customers for sharing. For example, you can earn more space on Dropbox if you refer friends and they sign up for an account. Or you can get a LivingSocial deal for free if you share it and three of your friends buy it.

> ### Dropbox
>
> Dropbox is a file storage and file-sharing service that lets you keep files in the cloud and access them on multiple devices. Founder Drew Houston originally applied to Y Combinator for the summer 2007 program, and he was accepted and told to bring on a cofounder. He brought on Arash Ferdowsi, and together they've built one of Y Combinator's most successful startups. Based in San Francisco, Dropbox has raised more than $250 million and had 175 million users as of July 2013.

Putting All Your Marketing Together

Using all these methods and channels in a lean way—from social media to content marketing to e-mail—you test and iterate in order to hone in on the right set of customers and ensure you're communicating the right value proposition to them via the right channels.

So how do you pull all this together? Understand where you are now with your analytics, and set goals for improvement on specific numbers. Track which channels bring in the most customers for the least amount of time and money. Track new customers and repeat customers. Activities happening on your site should be accounted for with a number or metric.

Just remember that you don't have to do everything. Figure out what's right for your business and goals and go after that.

For a list of marketing tools, check out http://tech.co/book.

The Harsh Reality

As much as you want it to, sometimes your marketing just doesn't work. And if your marketing isn't working, it might be because you haven't hit on the right product or found the right product-market fit. If your product is subpar or if consumers can't understand the need for it, you're going to have a really difficult time selling it and being successful. Yet even good marketing efforts won't always go viral, like you hope.

Even worse, sometimes you offend people with your marketing efforts. Groupon learned this lesson after being called offensive and racist for its 2011 Super Bowl ad, which started as an apparent plea for Tibet's plight and turned into advertising for the company's daily deals.

Along the way, you'll also run into marketing crises. For example, on February 15, 2011, a Red Cross employee—obviously having a lot of fun—accidentally broadcasted this tweet from @RedCross rather than her personal account: "Ryan found two more 4 bottle packs of Dogfish Head's Midas Touch beer … when we drink we do it right

#gettngslizzerd." The tweet was sent using HootSuite, which viewers could see. HootSuite knew this could spell major bad press for them.

So HootSuite flew into action with two parts charity and one dash of humor, donating to the Red Cross, encouraging others to donate, and sending a care package with a beer koozie to the mistweeter. Soon, with support from Dogfish Head, breweries were offering a free pint of beer for customers who donated a pint of blood to the Red Cross, rallying around the hashtag #gettngslizzerd. And soon afterward, Hoot-Suite launched tools for secure profiles—an extra step to confirm that you want to tweet from a protected account. What could have been a fiasco (and was for a short time) turned into a public relations boon for three companies. We have no idea what happened to the tweeter.

When Eddie Earnest launched seedRef in 2013, he started by calling it a "Klout score for your character" but quickly figured out that wasn't working. Now, he explains it more simply: a Web-based recruiting application. "It's safe to say that the first few iterations of my marketing copy were awful," says founder Eddie Earnest. "I actually think I was confusing myself along the way. I knew it was bad when I found myself having to spend massive amounts of time explaining who we were, what we did, and why it's useful. As we've grown, we've worked really hard on capturing the elements of a good story that seem to resonate with people."

That's why it's crucial to sit down and pull together your story. Cathy Brooks, a storyteller extraordinaire who spent 20 years in the tech industry doing events, media, public relations, and marketing, left a startup in May 2013 and

Cathy Brooks

With a background in journalism and public relations, Cathy Brooks is a storyteller. She spent 20 years in the tech industry, where her work included business development at Seesmic and producing the LeWeb conference in Paris. After a chance meeting with Tony Hsieh, she moved to downtown Vegas to pursue her other passion: dogs. At the end of 2013, she opened a private park and training academy called the Hydrant Club, funded by the Downtown Project.

decided to take the summer to figure out her own personal story. She talked to companies such as Intel and Microsoft, said yes to almost all conversations, and finally decided to move to Vegas and start the Hydrant Club, a dog park and training center—not exactly the story she had imagined, but one that was true to her passion and purpose.

"Storytelling is probably one of the most misunderstood and overused words in marketing today," she says. The problem is that companies think they're telling stories when they actually aren't. A real story requires a significant investment of time to figure out. "What I would encourage you to do is think about what you're doing on a daily basis, think about the stories you're telling," she says. "Take a minute to pause and step back from it."

Celebrate: Enjoy the Journey

South by Southwest (SXSW) Interactive in Austin, Texas, takes place every March and has become known for big marketing stunts. Brands large and small compete to host the most fun and awesome events. Although attendees go there to learn, network, and celebrate being a techie, it's also the place that helps launch new startups.

Twitter first started to catch people's attention at SXSW in 2007. In 2009, Foursquare was the talk of the town. The Foursquare team set up a literal game of foursquare outside the convention center, and attendees could get a T-shirt by playing a game. Someone created a venue on the Foursquare app called SXSW Foursquare Court, and the rest is history. And I'm sure the Foursquare team had fun that day; it wasn't a boring, promotional marketing stunt.

> ### South by Southwest (SXSW)
>
> SXSW is a huge annual festival that attracts tens of thousands of attendees each year. It started in 1987 with a focus on music, and film and interactive were added in 1994. The interactive component is what attracts startups and entrepreneurs, who spend their time at SXSW looking for press, building relationships, and attending awesome parties. SXSW takes place in Austin, Texas, a city with an eclectic culture that appeals to nonconformist artists and rebellious geeks alike.

ParkMe took a risk at SXSW 2012 by tagging cars with fake parking tickets and boots—and it paid off. The company booted 500 cars and also included a notice to the driver (pasted on the window) instructing them to download the app and put the boot on someone else's car. The notice read: "Damaging this device is not punishable by law … but it will affect your parking karma." They used the hashtag #bootedinaustin to spread and track the conversation on social media channels. As a result, they were mentioned on Channel 7 news. Was it clever? Yep. And once the booted car owner read the notice, it was also pretty funny.

Marketing is where you can really celebrate your uniqueness, whether you're selling a mobile app or cheap razor blades. Dollar Shave Club created a viral video that launched its razor blade product, featuring a toddler shaving a guy's head, a dancing bear, and a brash slogan: "Our blades are f***ing great." Then, they did it again with One Wipe Charlies, "butt wipes for men." The company found its preferred marketing medium and knocked it out of the park with humor. In watching the videos, you can tell this quirky humor is just expressing the personality and style of the founder.

Final Thoughts

There are lots of marketing tips and tactics you can follow, and you probably have tons of ideas and questions. The most important take-away for telling your story is to understand your *why*. If you know your *why*, it will be easier to tell a clear and compelling story. Stories with a strong *why* are easier to understand and easier to share because they capture people's hearts and convictions. Sweetgreen followed its *why* of living the sweet life in creating the Sweetlife Festival. Once you have your *why* story, the rest falls into place.

Even though you're creating a brand, being human is what it comes down to. If customers like you and feel affinity for your purpose, they'll be much more forgiving of the errors, missteps, and bugs that are bound to happen along the way.

13 Sales

You don't close a sale; you open a relationship if you want to build a long-term, successful enterprise.

—Patricia Fripp

In October 2013, the Dwolla payment network launched its new Dwolla Credit product with 47 partners. All those 47 businesses—which include Fiverr, Namecheap, Manpacks, and Tikly—were already set up to accept the new form of payment and had signed on to Dwolla's vision.

The vision was to be a business-friendly alternative to credit cards that could be used to buy everything from cheap Web design to domain names to underwear. Instead of paying a standard percentage fee, merchants accepting Dwolla Credit would pay only $0.25—or nothing for transactions under $10. How did they get nearly 50 businesses to sign on before launch?

It all started a year earlier, back in 2012. Dwolla's chief executive officer (CEO), Ben Milne, was talking with Alliance Data Systems, which now manages Dwolla's credit infrastructure, and handed them off to Alexander Taub, who worked on Dwolla's business development and partnerships. Taub's job was to continue negotiations and get a contract signed as fast as possible. They ended up inking a deal in the first quarter of 2013.

"Most of the high-level terms were agreed upon, but like any partnership with a publicly traded company, there were a million other things that needed to be worked on," wrote Taub, in a blog post on Medium.

With that settled, now it was time to start signing up partners. Taub and another Dwolla employee created the Dwolla Credit Pipeline, a list of people they wanted to partner with. Starting with the team's personal contacts, they ended up listing 100 to 200 companies. From there, they hired a business development and research intern to find companies in sectors they weren't familiar with. The goal was to find 25 partners for launch.

After celebrating July 4, Dwolla started having calls and meetings to get the deals signed. All in all, the team probably had 200 to 400 meetings in order to close those 47 partners, Taub recounts. After each meeting, they would send a follow-up e-mail with their pitch deck, which included what Dwolla Credit is, why it's exciting, who it's for, what you need to do to get involved, the time frame, and next steps. They started with safe partners—friends whom they knew well—in order to test out and refine their pitch and process from start to close.

The Dwolla team was successful because they understood how sales works. Just like building a startup, it's an iterative process: you have to hone in on your pitch, delivery, and process over time. *Over time* is an operative phrase here: sales don't happen overnight. It took Dwolla more than a year to form all the partnerships necessary to make Dwolla Credit happen. And relationships are key. Starting with people you know is how you make those initial sales, and then you can use those sales as proof of your credibility to other prospects.

Dwolla's sales process involved creating partnerships for a launch to signal to the market that it was a trusted brand. After launch, it continued selling to bring on new merchants. But your sales may be different: you may be selling your software directly to consumers. Or you might be a media company like Tech Cocktail, in which case you're selling audience engagement through online advertising and event sponsorships.

For this chapter, I'll talk about sales as those one-on-one interactions where you try to gain a customer or partner. I'll go over what the typical sales process looks like and what your attitude toward sales should be.

Although sales and marketing are related, they have distinct purposes. The goal of marketing is to communicate your message to the world, building relationships and gaining attention. Marketing is a broader activity than sales; sales refers to doing deals: convincing someone they should work with you. Often, marketing teams will generate leads—for example, Dwolla's marketing team might notice which companies retweet their blog posts—then send those leads to the sales team to close a deal. The sales team also comes up with their own leads through research, also called sales prospecting.

Before diving in, take a moment to think about your higher-level goals. What role does sales play in your organization? Is your product something that users can find and sign up for (and pay for) on their own, or do you need to be actively selling it and meeting with customers? Even if you don't sell directly to customers, could you benefit from creating partnerships with other businesses or thought leaders? Do you create any secondary products (such as reports or other content) that someone might like to sponsor? These are all reasons to hone your sales skills.

Sales Process

You'll have to tweak this model to fit your startup, but here's what a traditional sales process looks like.

- *Lead generation:* Initially, you want to figure out who your target is. Dwolla decided to focus on companies with fewer than 5,000 transactions a month (since it was launching in beta), small to medium lifestyle businesses, and funded startups. You're looking for users who have the needs you're addressing—for Dwolla, those small businesses feel the pain of credit card fees more than their corporate counterparts. One way to generate leads is to see what type of people or companies are visiting your website.

- *Qualify leads:* This is where you take all the leads you've generated—for Dwolla, that list of 100 to 200 people they knew combined with the research from their intern—and rank them to figure out whom to contact first. Our vice president of sales and business development, Steve Kann, ranks leads based on the contact's job title, the company size, and what industry the person is in. Following are a few examples of other ranking criteria that different startups use.

Social Tables, mentioned earlier in the book, was a consumer product that decided to go enterprise and sell its event planning solution to hotels and other venues. With a sales team of about four people, they spent 2013 signing up venues. They used the popular BANT criteria for ranking leads, which stands for budget, authority, need, and timeline. In other words, they looked for contacts who had a large budget, were in charge of making the purchasing decision, desperately needed the product, and might sign a deal soon.

One helpful tip from HubSpot is to analyze past leads who converted into customers and figure out what actions they took before they converted. How much interaction did they have with you before deciding to buy? That way, you can figure out the best time to approach a lead and try to make a sale without wasting your time or annoying people.

At Curbed Network, which owns the three blogs *Curbed, Racked,* and *Eater,* sales involves getting paid to syndicate their content out to other sites. *Curbed* is quite successful, reaching more than 5 million unique visitors per month, so it actually gets a lot of inbound requests to syndicate content. Then, it's the team's job to rank those leads. To do that, cofounder and vice president of strategic development Alexis Juneja relies on her strict syndication criteria. She tells the lead what those criteria are—such as guidelines for how the content must be displayed—and then simply says no to everyone who won't comply. Part of qualifying leads is figuring out whom to delete from your list.

Alexis Juneja

Alexis Juneja was the cofounder of Curbed Network, a media company that includes three sites: *Curbed,* showcasing real estate and design; *Eater,* featuring dining and nightlife; and *Racked,* focusing on shopping and fashion. Curbed grew to more than 35 million page views per month and 50 employees before being acquired by Vox Media in November 2013. Juneja is now a vice president at Vox Media. She comes to the startup and media world from a background in finance.

- *Research:* Always know your audience. The pitch to one person isn't the same as the pitch to another. The last thing you want to do is get a big meeting with an important sales prospect and come across unprepared or try to sell the person something that's not relevant. So before you contact your leads, do some research so you can tailor your pitch. Create a profile of all leads. This is where you store any and all information about interactions they've had with you: which forms they completed, which e-mails they opened, how they interacted with you on social media, and which pages they visited on your site.

- *Initial contact:* When you first talk with a lead, your goal is to listen—starting with the moment the person picks up the phone. Learn about the person's needs, wants, reservations, and obstacles. Only then can you figure out if your product or service will be a good fit. But don't hide the fact that you're looking to make a sale. Instead, build rapport by getting the person to agree with you. For example, you might say, "I'm sure you care about improving in this area"—who could say no to that? When the person talks, make sure that you've understood correctly by paraphrasing the ideas and confirming your interpretation.

  As the call winds up, try to set up another appointment for a more formal proposal. And be clear on what the prospect's goals are. "Always ask what success means to the 'decision maker.' If you don't realize or ask what *wins* look like to your customers, then you will never understand how to create ROI [return on investment]," says Clarisa Lindenmeyer, vice president of public relations at the accelerator Tech Wildcatters. Show that ROI clearly when you make your formal proposal.

Sales Tips

Sales is a delicate dance of building relationships and doing business transactions. Even if you're an introverted techie, you have to do it yourself early on. Here are some principles to keep in mind along the way.

- *Start by selling yourself.* Before you sell your product, you have to sell yourself as someone who's likeable and trustworthy. That starts the minute you tweet or shake hands with someone. Be friendly and interested, and don't dive right into your pitch.

- *Focus on the prospect.* It's all about your prospect. Find out what the prospect is really looking to do. What are his or her goals? One of Tech Cocktail's early business development leads, Mary Ellen Delaney, reminds herself to be present in the moment, listening and focusing on what the other person is saying while figuring out how she can help him or her.

    Steve approaches sales by caring. I know that probably sounds simplistic, but the person you're talking to can tell when you don't care. Listen to the words the person uses when describing his or her needs and problems, and articulate your value in those words.

    In the end, he says, you also feel better about doing sales. You aren't the greasy car salesperson: you're the respectful collaborator who isn't afraid to say when your product isn't a good fit. "If you focus on relationships and not transactions, you'll get both," Steve says.

- *Show testimonials.* In sales, as in many other domains, we need social proof. Trying out something untested is scary; trying out something that famous people recommend makes good sense. Particularly when you have a small startup, prospects won't want to take a chance on you, have it turn out badly, and be held accountable by their bosses. Offering testimonials and explaining who else uses your product eases their concern.

    For example, .CO was starting a completely new top-level domain, and they knew it would be a huge challenge to get the first customers to join. Why would anyone want a .CO when no one knew what a .CO was? So they started looking for anchor tenants who would prove the worth of .CO to everyone else. And they got them, including Twitter (t.co), AngelList (angel.co), and 500 Startups (500.co). "The ROI on getting early adopters that are notable and credible is exponentially higher than anything else we've ever done," says founder Juan Diego Calle. Obviously Tech Cocktail (tech.co) was a pretty smart partnership, too.

- *Volume, volume, volume.* Once you've qualified and ranked your leads, it's time to get down to business. Often, the way to win in sales is just to contact as many prospects as possible.

  Steve recommends keeping track of your performance and setting a goal for a certain number of calls to make per day. For example, say that out of every 100 outbound e-mails, you get 11 responses. Five of those have a real interest and request a proposal, and one ends up buying your product for $1,500. If your goal is to sell $7,500 per day, you know that you need to send 500 e-mails. Once you have those goals, share them with your team—and try to beat them!

- *Be patient.* Research by Gleanster suggests that 30 to 50 percent of leads are not ready to buy when they enter your sales pipeline. Getting a yes can take months. When I talked to Mary Ellen about this chapter, she had just closed a deal that was a full year in the making.

- *Iterate.* As we saw with Dwolla, tweaking and changing your pitch is the way to perfect it over time. You can even collaborate with the marketing team on iteration. For example, say that most of their leads from e-book downloads end up becoming customers, but few of their leads from Twitter do. That can help the marketing side refine their own initiatives and experiment with new ways of generating leads.

- *Create a sales culture.* Everyone that the team meets could be a potential prospect or friend of a prospect—and the business will make more money if all employees keep that in mind. Everyone knows other people; if you create a sales culture, then there should never be a shortage of leads that could turn to sales.

Cofounder Neil Patel of KISSmetrics recommends hiring salespeople who are comfortable with change and uncertainty. He says they should be "hunters": people who can find their own leads rather than just attacking the ones you feed them. They should also be "mavericks," trailblazers who can educate prospects on your innovative idea and come up with their own processes.

For a list of sales tools, check out http://tech.co/book.

The Harsh Reality

Sales is a skill you will use across all aspects of your company. As soon as you decided to become a founder, guess what? You became a salesperson. You are selling your concept continually, whether it's to sell product directly, gain the best employees, bring on partners or investors, or pitch press. Get used to it. It's now a part of your daily job.

"I always looked at sales as such a foreign thing … I never considered I would have anything to do with it. But when I started working with Frank to build Tech Cocktail, it was the first big challenge I had to take on. We had to—there wasn't anyone else and we didn't have any funding," reflects my chief operating officer Jen. She continues:

> I started testing pitches everywhere. I remember reaching out to this great guy I had met at one of our events who suggested we might be able to work together. He introduced me to someone who introduced me to someone else—eventually I got to understand their needs and got a proposal in the right hands. It seemed like it took forever. I was in a San Francisco hotel with terrible reception when I got the call that they liked my proposal and would sponsor four of our major events. I was literally running around the lobby trying to get signal. When I closed that deal, I almost cried. I did a happy dance right there in the lobby.

The reality is, sales is a complicated process, and it will be a big learning curve for most people. And the difficulties start the moment you begin.

The problem with sales is that you're dealing with human beings, human relationships, and often complex organizations. You may be talking to someone, only to realize that that person doesn't have the authority within the company to approve the deal. But you can't just come right out and say, "Are you allowed to sign off on this? If not, who should I talk to?" That would bruise egos and ruin your chances of an introduction. So probe and ask polite questions, even if you feel impatient.

Testimonials are crucial, but how do you sign on your first customer? It's the same problem as getting your first job: you *need* experience, but you *can't get* experience because you *have no* experience. That means you might have to give things away for free in the beginning.

"I've been shut down many times or have been told to just 'leave a business card' when cold-pitching to companies to solicit our services. They needed to see proof of our work, and we didn't have anything but our passion and promises," says Jeromy Ko, a social media strategist at the Social Firm.

When you do sales, you'll need to thicken up your skin. "You are going to get nine nos before you get a yes—you're going to get 99 nos before you get a yes," says Mary Ellen. Now is not the time for big egos or pride; it's the time to recognize the harsh reality that people aren't as interested in your product as you think they should be.

Since you get so many nos, it's absolutely crucial that you're constantly pushing forward. Always be hungry. The worst thing for a sales team is stagnation—a problem Social Tables faced in early 2013. Ram Parimi, who leads sales for Social Tables, was alarmed to notice that the team wasn't moving fast enough; somehow, they had created a culture where it was okay to make fewer and fewer calls per day.

"What we were missing out on by lack of effort—that's something that is very dangerous in sales and needs to be corrected quickly," he says. He was forced to set ambitious goals and make it clear to everyone that minimal effort wasn't cutting it; they each had be making 60 to 80 calls per day.

Part of the problem was the small sales team. Without a room of 20 people buzzing with phone calls, you just don't feel that competition to beat your peers. So in a startup, you have to cultivate a sense of urgency yourself. "You can't be comfortable doing whatever it is you're doing—you have to triple that," Parimi says.

One way that sales teams slow down is by getting tunnel vision. It's when the team gets the slightest hint of an opportunity, holds onto it for dear life, and stops focusing so much on all their other leads. Joanne Black, author of *Pick Up the Damn Phone!*, made this mistake when she was one of two finalists to sign a million-dollar deal. And she lost it.

"I'd already envisioned how I would spend my commission and the accolades I would receive from my firm," she says. "The bigger mistake, however, was putting all my eggs in one basket. Not only did I lose the deal, but I had been so focused on getting this client's business that I neglected prospecting. Suddenly I had no pipeline. It was a harsh lesson I've never forgotten. I will never again let my pipeline dry up like that. No matter how busy we are, we must always be prospecting."

Celebrate: Enjoy the Journey

The sales bell is one of the most iconic examples of celebration at a startup. Who isn't going to want to make that sales bell ring?

InsightSquared rings a sales bell when they sign a new customer, and everyone stops for a moment and listens to the sales representative, who starts by describing how the whole team contributed to the deal. Tech Cocktail also has a sales bell installed in our office, and it rings every time we sell advertising, gain new sponsorships, or ink new partnerships. Everyone looks forward to ringing it because they know how important sales are to the future of the company—but it also has a fun element to it, which is in line with our core values.

The sales bell takes advantage of the inherent competitiveness in all of us, which is another excellent motivator and fuel for celebration. Competition was a major part of the way that Social Tables got out of its own rut. The team created a picture of a puzzle covered up by blocks and broadcasted it onto a big screen in the office. Whenever someone made a sale, one block was removed. Every time a whole row of blocks was removed, the team went down to a nearby bar and took a shot or had a beer.

To incentivize the team, Parimi also took deals he personally closed and awarded the credit to other team members based on high performance—like making the most calls in a day. That way, the team was motivated to put in more and more effort, whatever the outcome.

"It became a culture of everybody helping each other and everybody trying to be number one," he says. And it worked. In September 2012, after just pivoting to an enterprise company, Social Tables had zero sales. In 2013, it onboarded more than 1,000 clients and saw 20 to 25 percent month-over-month growth in revenue.

"Sales at startups has become both interesting, fun, and actually quite challenging. Once you figure out the method to the madness, it becomes one of the most fun jobs in the world," says Parimi.

Celebrating money is great—it's what keeps you alive as a company. But on top of that, you can celebrate the relationships you're forging. Relationships aren't transactional. Even if you don't make a sale, handling yourself gracefully and being a decent person will have benefits down the road.

Final Thoughts

At Dwolla, the fun started right from the moment Taub was introduced to his contact at Alliance Data Systems, the fundamental partner who would make the other 47 partnerships possible. Milne sent that introduction, and the subject line was "My favorite introduction ever."

Dwolla's partners also joined in with the spirit of fun and celebration, the idea that together they were blazing a path that would have awesome results for consumers. WunWun, for example, celebrated its partnership announcement with Dwolla by giving customers 3 percent off all Dwolla Credit transactions.

As for Taub, launching Dwolla Credit—after all his hard work building partnerships—was a moment of pride. "This has been the most exhilarating and stressful time of my life," he says. "I've never been part of something so big."

Part 5
Money

14 Bootstrapping

I am a bootstrapper. I have initiative and insight and guts, but not much money. I will succeed because my efforts and my focus will defeat bigger and better-funded competitors. I am fearless.

—Seth Godin,
"Bootstrapper's Manifesto"

What is bootstrapping? Leveraging yourself, undertaking something with no outside help, being self-initiated and self-sustaining. Or the original definition: pulling on boots with no help from others, using just your own efforts and strength. It's real life for entrepreneurs.

Bootstrapping is what most people do when starting their business. Maybe you use your personal savings or take on credit card debt until you become profitable enough to create a sustainable business. Bootstrapping can be a long-term plan or a strategy for the initial stages before seeking investment. With no outside funding, you become laser-focused on creating a prototype and finding your business some traction.

It's often said that 99 percent of businesses are bootstrapped. From Basecamp to GitHub to Plenty of Fish, plenty of startups are bootstrapped and proud. Entrepreneur Ryan Carson, the creator of DropSend and Treehouse, estimates that you can feasibly create enterprise Web apps for less than $50,000.

I've started a few different companies that all began bootstrapped. Tech Cocktail was proudly bootstrapped for its first seven-plus years. Early on, we used free or low-cost software solutions to get the job done. Our first event registration service was literally a comment string on a blog post. We bartered to get free services for our early newsletters, analytics, and social media management. Our first event even took advantage of free, donated wine and family and friends as alcohol pourers and guest greeters. It doesn't get more bootstrapped than that.

I've always admired fellow Chicagoan Jason Fried's bootstrapping approach. Fried started his consulting company, then called 37signals, in 1999. In 2004, his company built the project management tool Basecamp to improve its own productivity and collaboration. Two years later, the company rolled out a group chat application called Campfire and then a contact manager called Highrise. They bootstrapped the entire time with the mind-set that you need to practice *making* money, not spending it.

"This whole tech world is not focused on that, and that is a dangerous, dangerous thing," says Fried, who believes that being short on cash makes you hungrier. Some startups forget revenue amid the glamor of being an entrepreneur and the glitz of raising funding. They forget that survival is the only thing they should be focused on.

"I'm a big fan of the idea of longevity—just sticking it out. If you manage to stick around, you get successful," Fried explained to me once—and I couldn't agree more. Sometimes, entrepreneurs don't have enough passion for the idea to be patient with their journey. There are very few overnight successes, despite what startup lore would have you believe.

As a bootstrapper, Fried believes in having fewer employees. He says, "We work really hard not to hire people. We rarely hire. We hire like a couple people a year." Today, Basecamp is 15 years old and has just over 40 employees. Hiring less puts less pressure on your company, since you're not covering the costs of more and more salaries. "I would rather feel the pain of hiring someone a little bit too late than too early," explains Fried.

For the people he does hire, Fried believes that expensive perks and benefits are less important than giving them interesting and inspiring work to do. And most of the Basecamp team is remote, so they don't have to splurge on a huge office. They also don't spend money on marketing, except the time employees take to blog.

Jason Fried and Basecamp are leaders of the bootstrapping movement, which has rallied many entrepreneurs together around the cause of being independent. The barriers to starting up a Web or mobile software company have come down significantly over the past decade, making it possible to bootstrap. Thanks in part to the dropping costs of cloud storage and hardware, as well as the proliferation of open source software, you can start a company for far less money than ever before.

Bootstrapping is complementary to the lean startup practices I discussed earlier in this book. The lean startup approach doesn't necessarily involve bootstrapping, but lean startup practices are conducive to spending little money and keeping costs down.

Bootstrapping Tips

Here are some tips for saving money while bootstrapping:

- *Moonlight first.* Starting out, you might want to keep your day job or go part-time. This may sound counter to the *just do it* tone of the rest of the book, but if you're bootstrapping, you need to somehow fund your efforts. Keep in mind that things always take longer and cost more than you expect—and you'd rather not discover that after you quit your job and run out of money. Carson of Treehouse believes you should always plan to be 10 percent over budget and three months behind schedule.

- *Barter and negotiate.* Get in the habit of asking for things in exchange for your services. You may not want to waste your valuable time on doing services for other people, but you have a better supply of time than money when bootstrapping.

  Think about what you can offer others that they cannot refuse (within legal parameters—I'm not talking about selling your organs). Lawyers, accountants, printers, landlords, designers, developers—figure out how you can help them and talk to them about ways to work together. For example, an accountant might need a new website, and you could create one in exchange for accounting services.

  Keep in mind that everything in this world is negotiable if you approach it from the right angle. Every time you go to spend money, ask yourself if negotiation is possible. Maybe you can lower the price or convince the seller to throw in something extra. "Make a point of telling everyone except for your users/buyers/clients that you're bootstrapping. You'll be amazed what people will do and the discounts they'll give to help you," says Kelly Fallis, chief executive officer (CEO) of Remote Stylist.

- *Cut expenses.* What is the bare minimum you can live on and still get your job done? That is the question you need to ask yourself—and then make the appropriate changes to your lifestyle to cut expenses. On the business side, Carson of Treehouse recommends that you skip the business cards and recruit friends as usability testers. Similarly, when you run into problems, Basecamp recommends cutting back on scope or features rather than increasing budget. Slimming down the project could get you to a launching point without blowing the bank. And always be on the lookout for ways you can automate processes.

- *Get creative.* As a bootstrapper, you'll need to discover unique ways to save money. For example, when Patrick J. Sweeney II of dwinQ was building ServerVault, he needed bandwidth but didn't want to pay expensive setup and termination charges. He had a friend who owned a data center, so Sweeney rented the office next door to his. He recalls, "We literally crawled through the ceiling with a Cat-5 cable, and I hopped onto his huge bandwidth feed. I paid him only for what I used and saved myself thousands." That same friend wanted to hire someone to get rid of old office furniture, so Sweeney got paid to take it off his hands. "The lesson is: if you want something, figure out how to get it for free. If you can get it for free, figure out how to get someone to pay you to take it," says Sweeney. Great lesson—and exactly the creative thinking you need to be a successful bootstrapped company.

  Cheek'd is a dating product where you give people you'd like to date little black cards with fun sayings, such as "I'm totally cooler than your date" or "I'm free this weekend." The company was boot-strapped for three and a half years, working out of coffee shops and at home. Founder Lori Cheek came up with lots of (free) guerilla marketing tactics: she chalked the website address on sidewalks and slipped Cheek'd cards into random people's pockets, hoods, and bags. She used up her savings, then turned to her closet to sell her designer clothes for additional money. She also rented out her apartment on Airbnb and sold electronics and other belongings. "I've done everything I know how to do, and ultimately, I've built a brand and a company and thousands of people are using the service," says Cheek. "It's the most rewarding feeling."

What a Bootstrapped Startup Looks Like

Those ideas are all nice, but how do you put them into practice? Here's what bootstrapping looks like in all the different elements of your business.

- *Team:* Initially you probably won't have the cash flow to pay a bunch of employees full-time. First, decide if you need them full-time—you may be able to get by with some part-time contractors until you start bringing in consistent cash flow. Another option would be to offer equity rather than a salary (do your equity research first!). Also consider hiring great people with less experience—who cost less—and then training them. Or, you might outsource to a country where labor is much cheaper.

  You can always ask for help by going more public with your request. Find interns, volunteers, friends, and family to start. When Jen and I first started taking Tech Cocktail on full-time, we were living in the same building in two different condos. We decided to cut our burn in half by sharing one unit. Lots of entrepreneurs take this approach and decide to live together.

- *Marketing:* Focus on content marketing and word of mouth as your cheapest options. (See Chapter 12 for more details.)

- *Workspace:* Do you *need* an office? For free, you could work from home, coffee shops, the library, or a local college or university. For cheap, you could upgrade to coworking or shared space. If you do get an office, remember that leases are negotiable—ask to pay less now and more later, get the landlord to throw in furniture, or negotiate a month free.

- *Legal:* Clint Costa, an attorney at Harrison & Held, suggests negotiating a fixed fee for entity formation. I've done this before—and
because entity formation is generally a simple task, it makes more
sense. Whether or not that works, ask your lawyer for a work plan
with specific tasks and time/cost estimates. Some lawyers may even
do work pro bono, take an IOU, or barter if they think you're a
promising business and they want to earn your loyalty. I'm finding
more law firms taking this approach with early-stage startups—after
all, they don't really make much money on early-stage startups
anyway.

    Also, the more organized you are, the less time your lawyer will
waste on the clock trying to sift through your disorganization.

- *Reward programs:* Bootstrappers love taking advantage of reward
programs. From credit cards that offer money back or points for
free travel to programs like some of our partners offer, you can save
a lot of money. For example, if you have a .CO domain, you have
access to resources at go.co, including promotion, networking, and
education. .CO offers things like free tickets to Startup Weekends,
Google AdWords credit, search engine optimization (SEO) con-
sultations, free or discounted coworking space access, and public
relations help. And American Airlines runs a free program called
Business Extra. If you sign up for the program, your company earns
points for travel awards when booking flights on American, while
your employees also earn AAdvantage miles.

For a list of bootstrapping tools, check out http://tech.co/book.

The Harsh Reality

Bootstrapping can be very rewarding, but it's not easy. It's a mind-set,
and one that's sometimes difficult to maintain over time. Jen and I
worked from home or from friends' office for years, used our savings to
pay employees during a couple of tough times, and often worked seven

days a week with very little downtime. There were definitely stressful times where we had to remind each other why we were hanging on to our dream.

Chase Boulter, cofounder and CEO of the bootstrapped company Titan Analytics, has been bootstrapping businesses since the age of 12 (he's now in his early 20s). "Bootstrapping is difficult. There is no other way to put it. When you reach that final sprint to release your product or service and the cash cushions that you and your cofounders have put away start to dry up, you really start to feel that determination (and stress) start to kick in. You have everything riding on this business. Your life, possessions, reputation, and so much more are at jeopardy," says Boulter. "It is a harsh reality that many cannot survive this pressure cooker. For those who do, I can tell you that it will be one of the most rewarding and paralyzing experiences of your life."

There may be days when you aren't able to pay the people helping you out, let alone yourself. Or there might be days when a customer doesn't pay you on time or decides to not pay you at all after you performed a service. Unexpected costs may arise that drain your account. Or some things may take 10 times longer than you estimated. Just like climbing a mountain or running a marathon, bootstrapping is something you need to prepare yourself for mentally. Don't wait until the shit hits the fan.

There's a great book about how to prepare for hiking the Appalachian Trail called *Appalachian Trials,* written by former Tech Cocktail team member Zach Davis, that we can learn a lot from. Davis believes that the difference between finishing the 2,200-mile Appalachian Trail and not finishing is almost all mental. The first month on the trail, you encounter hardships, but everything is still new—the pure excitement and adrenaline get you through it. It's actually the next two to seven months of hiking that beat you down. At some point, you inevitably ask yourself, "Why am I doing this?"

While bootstrapping your company, you feel the same excitement during the first few months. Each day you feel the energy that comes with the freedom of sailing your own ship; you bask in a newly discovered creative rush. But this is a marathon, my friend, not a sprint—and you have to be mentally ready for the long term. Before you start, take a page from Davis's book and make a list (adapted for our purposes) called "I am starting my company because … " and focus on why you're doing this. Here are some examples to get you going:

I am starting my company because …

> I don't want to work for anyone else.
> I see this problem and want to solve it so no one else has to have this problem anymore.
> I believe my ideas are important and should be explored.
> I believe there is a better way to live and this will allow me to do it.
> I believe in building a sustainable business that helps make the world a better place.

You get the idea. *The purpose of this list is to give you purpose.* Post it on your wall. Have it handy whenever you feel down or are in a rough spot. "When I'm having a bad day, when it's raining, I just come back to, Why am I doing this stuff? And who am I working with? And that just brightens me up because I feel lucky," says Jenn Lim, CEO and chief happiness officer of Delivering Happiness.

Jenn Lim

As a consultant for Zappos, Jenn Lim created its famous Culture Book in 2005 and has produced it annually since. In 2010, she helped Tony Hsieh launch and market his book *Delivering Happiness: A Path to Profits, Passion, and Purpose.* They did a cross-country bus tour, then spun off a separate company called Delivering Happiness. Lim now runs it as CEO and chief happiness officer, and the company offers events, coaching for businesses, and inspiration to make the world a happier place. Before Zappos, Lim worked as a consultant in the digital, writing, and graphic design industries.

Boulter agrees that startups are a mental game. He urges you to "prepare yourself mentally for the process. It will take a lot of will to power through those tough times when you are strapped for cash and have $1,000 in the bank to last ... the month."

For example, Collis Ta'eed and his wife spent all their savings and credit lines on starting Envato, an ecosystem of sites that help people be creative. In the process, they got kicked out of their house and lived with their in-laws, then borrowed money from their parents to keep their dream alive. "When we finally launched our first product, we were running on fumes! It was very humbling and rather terrifying. But we got some early sales, kept doing freelance work to keep the lights on, and eventually things took off," remembers Ta'eed.

So if you're planning on bootstrapping, just be ready—it won't be a walk in the park. Bootstrapping is an up-and-down roller coaster as you bring your dream to life. You'll likely be making sacrifices for weeks, months, and sometimes years. Perseverance, patience, and a calm mind will help you through the tougher times.

Celebrate: Enjoy the Journey

Bootstrapping may be hard, but it doesn't mean you can't celebrate and have some fun along the way. In fact, *it's all the more reason to make sure you are enjoying the journey!* I remember back in college when I didn't have a real job or real income yet, but I was able to make do with what I had—great friends and experiences. And you can do the latter economically.

When Jen and I took our Kauai workation, we did it on the cheap. We used airline miles for free flights, and I negotiated a lower rate on a house because it was winter (rainy season) in a more rural area versus a touristy one. We hit the grocery store and made our own meals, saving us from paying resort food prices. At that time, I was personally writing five or more articles a day for the site. I posted this on my @FrankGruber Twitter account on December 10, 2010, at 1:16 PM Hawaii time:[1]

> Ok five articles written … break time … going to explore the island a bit. Aloha.

Taking a trip to Kauai might not make sense for you, but there are lots of options: head to a local beach, host a team talent show or bowling tournament, or go away for a long weekend in a nearby area. More simply, take some time to go for a walk and feel the sun on your face. Take a night off and be social. I'm very serious when I say that these minicelebrations of all sizes are critical to keeping your morale up and staying motivated as you hustle to get your business going.

Ta'eed of Envato had a tradition of taking a break by going to the mall, getting coffee, and talking over plans for the business. "It's such a feeling of possibility when you're starting out, and having cofounders (who in my case were my wife and best friend) is a really fun way to dream big together. Years later we still laugh about the days when the mall was our meeting room."

Aaron Schwartz of Modify Watches saves little pieces of customer feedback. He puts handwritten notes on the walls, and he also keeps a folder of nice e-mails. Every week, he sends an e-mail to the team with the latest positive customer feedback, delivering a little joy to their inboxes. It's celebration, at no cost at all.

Finally, celebrate living the dream and doing it on your own terms! Bootstrappers should be proud of themselves. There are sure to be big ups and downs, but the ups mean more to you when you're working for yourself.

---

[1] https://twitter.com/FrankGruber/status/11921920773591040

Final Thoughts

After launching Basecamp, Fried's company was approached by almost 30 venture capital firms wanting to invest. Finally, in 2006, he took funding from Jeff Bezos—not for the money, but for the wisdom. But Basecamp retains the bootstrapper ethos. Following in their footsteps should keep your company focused and not doing things just because you have the money to do them.

Fried believes the best way to celebrate while bootstrapping is to give people their paychecks. Beyond that, when they launch a new feature, Basecamp configures its software so a message is sent into their chat room whenever someone makes a purchase, alerting the team to the total sold since the feature launched. This gives everyone an intrinsic motivation boost and a feeling of progress.

"It's important to celebrate every sale, every customer's name, every customer's location, as much data as you can share with the rest of the company—let people know that this stuff is working. A lot of companies will have a cash register sound tied to their ordering system, and those little things really matter because people are working hard, and then they know their hard work is paying off. And that helps a lot more than a party," Fried explains.

Jeff Bezos

Jeff Bezos is the founder and CEO of Amazon. Founded in 1994, Amazon started as an online bookstore (its first book sold in July 1995 was *Fluid Concepts & Creative Analogies: Computer Models of the Fundamental Mechanisms of Thought*). Amazon's mission is to be "Earth's most customer-centric company where people can find and discover anything they want to buy online." The Seattle company went through an initial public offering (IPO) in 1997, launched the Kindle e-book reader in 2007, and debuted the Kindle Fire tablet in 2011. Amazon now has more than 97,000 employees and sells millions of products.

In 2000, Bezos founded a spaceflight startup called Blue Origin. Its goal is to make space travel cheaper and safer, and it's currently working on suborbital and orbital technology. In 2013, Bezos personally bought the *Washington Post* for $250 million.

15 Funding

Money is only a tool. It will take you wherever you wish, but it will not replace you as the driver.

—Ayn Rand

I n 2010, Tech Cocktail rented a house in Austin, Texas, during the SXSW Interactive conference. We had a few extra rooms, so we sublet our space to a couple of different sets of entrepreneurs. The team of Travis Kalanick and Ryan Graves were testing the concept of an on-demand black car service for the week, which would turn into UberCab and then eventually Uber. We sublet the other part of the house to New York–based entrepreneur Dave Lifson, who was starting a social media management platform called Postling. Lifson cofounded the startup with Chris Maguire and Haim Schoppik, cofounders of Etsy.

Lifson was on a mission at SXSW, and it was not to see how many Texas-shaped waffles he could find (although that is something to enjoy and be proud of—I love those Texas-shaped waffles). Instead, Lifson was on a mission to meet angel investors and raise seed funding for Postling.

Before SXSW, Lifson had created an AngelList application, sent it out, received a bunch of introductions, and been funded by David Rose and Chris Yeh. But Lifson knew that social media management tools were changing quickly, and they needed to change direction. So they pivoted, and then resent the AngelList application in hopes that the social proof of having investors would lure in a few more investors—and it did.

In Austin, Lifson wanted to meet with as many investors as he could. He leveraged some of his AngelList and personal connections to talk with Tom McInerney, who decided to fund the project after 30 minutes. McInerney then referred Lifson to Paige Craig, who was in and also pulled in Dave McClure. Once word spread, Thomas Korte joined and Lifson was introduced via e-mail to investor Kal Vepuri, who was also at SXSW. After meeting up in person, Vepuri was in. Lifson then met with our old pal Gary Vaynerchuk, who also joined. Techstars cofounder David Cohen finished off their round. In six days, this amounted to $200,000 raised in Austin alone, bringing Postling's total seed funding to $350,000.

I like to think we gave Lifson a little extra Tech Cocktail luck, since he stayed with us that year. But a few other things actually helped make Postling so fundable to all these angels. First, Postling had a great founding team, with experience building products at Amazon and Etsy. Second, by pivoting and changing their product focus, the founders had shown in their short existence as a company that they could respond to feedback quickly. Third, Lifson was able to quickly articulate a compelling vision backed by domain expertise.

Finally, Postling took advantage of the then-new AngelList to find and connect with angel investors. AngelList has since become the de facto way to raise angel funding. Lifson and his team also leveraged both online and offline networks to help build relationships, using Twitter, LinkedIn, and more. They didn't cold e-mail investors; the investors that signed on became supporters and gave them warm introductions to others.

This chapter looks at your funding options (beyond just the angels that Lifson used), how to pitch to investors, how to find the right investors for you, and how to structure the deal once it's finally in the works. Let's start by looking at different funding options.

Funding Options

- *Debt financing:* Bank loans are probably the most well-known debt financing option other than credit cards, but depending on the amount, they can be difficult to obtain as a new startup. Loans can be a good funding source when you need working capital or equipment. Working capital is funding to tide you over between customers ordering and you actually getting paid. And when you buy equipment (such as a server), the purchase acts as collateral; the bank can seize the server if you don't pay them back. Later-stage startup companies can secure a type of loan called venture debt, which is paid back after about three years. With bank loans, you keep your equity but pay interest. Other debt financing options include loans available from the Small Business Administration, accounts receivable lines of credit, and nonrecourse invoice factoring options (the latter two provide financing by converting accounts receivable to cash).

- *Government funding:* If you're a high-tech startup doing heavy research and development, check out options such as the Small Business Innovation Research grants ($150,000 to $1 million) through organizations such as the National Science Foundation and others, FederalGrants.com, and programs by your city or state government. The benefit of taking a government grant is that you don't have to give up equity. The downside is that it's very competitive. Another drawback is the timeline: most government programs have very strict schedules for submitting grant proposals and doling out funds. This window may be at least 90 days, which means you could apply and not hear anything for a few months.

- *Friends and family:* If you have friends and family willing to support your dream, then you might want to take them up on it. A friends and family round of funding is usually in the tens of thousands of dollars (although I once met a startup team in Dallas who raised a friends and family round of $6 million—I'd love to meet their friends and family!). Remember, they may not realize that most startups fail. Whatever amount they give you, make sure they can afford to lose it.

- *Angels:* Angel investors are a common starting point for equity funding. No, they don't have wings—but they can help give your startup wings. Angel investors are individuals who invest their own money, usually tens or hundreds of thousands of dollars. Angel investors who invest larger amounts are sometimes called super angels. In many cities, you'll find angel investor groups where angels get together to listen to pitches and make investments.

  Compared with venture capitalists (VCs), angels typically offer less complicated and friendlier terms for entrepreneurs.

That's partly because they invest for different reasons: whereas VCs are working to get a return for their own investors, angels often just want to give back and help the community. Getting angel funding can also be a faster process, as we saw with Postling. That said, angel investors will likely want some involvement in your company to help guide it toward success.

- *Venture capital:* If you're looking for millions of dollars in funding, the classic venture capitalist is whom you need to call. VC firms manage money from other people (called limited partners) and make a percentage of return based on the success of the fund's portfolio companies. If you go down this path, it's an entire world you'll need to study up on. Different VCs invest in different types of companies—by stage, geographic region, or industry. There are VCs with good reputations and those with bad ones. Many people compare the relationship with your VC to getting married, as you're tightly coupled with them for the long haul. VCs are looking for large returns in a fairly short timeline, so keep that in mind.

  In addition to money, your VC should be a valuable source of guidance and connections, which can help you tremendously. On the negative side, funding terms are usually more complicated and less entrepreneur-friendly than with angels, and most VCs want to be more involved in operations. Also, raising funding from VCs usually takes longer: they have a thorough due diligence process and just more cooks in the kitchen along the way.

- *Rewards-based crowdfunding:* With the rise of sites such as Kickstarter, Indiegogo, and many others, you can now get your startup idea funded by the masses. Crowdfunded products can raise anywhere from a few thousand dollars to millions of dollars. It's called rewards-based crowdfunding because your backers are rewarded with a small trinket that may range from a T-shirt to a copy of your product or creation to an exclusive experience, such as dinner with the founders.

Aside from the funding itself, crowdfunding is a great marketing tool and a way to validate your idea to future investors. The great part is that these rewards-based funding platforms do not give away equity in your company. Just understand that not all platforms are created equal. For example, Kickstarter is all or nothing, meaning if you don't meet your goal, you don't get any money, but Indiegogo allows you to keep anything you raise. On Kickstarter, 56 percent of projects fail, receiving zero funding.

Crowdfunding can generate lots of enthusiasm and support, but it can also generate backlash and annoyance if your product is delayed. You may raise more money than you intended, which means you'll have to ship more products—a good problem, but still a problem.

- *Equity-based crowdfunding:* Thanks to the Jumpstart Our Businesses Startups (JOBS) Act in the United States, entrepreneurs are now allowed to raise funding from nonaccredited investors (people with less than a $1 million net worth or $200,000 in annual income). Before, regulations would have made this kind of fund-raising prohibitively expensive and time-consuming. The JOBS Act was signed in April 2012, and the Securities and Exchange Commission (SEC) proposed rules for crowdfunding in October 2013. A comment period followed, and the official rules will likely go into effect spring 2014.

  Startups can raise up to $1 million per year under the crowdfunding rules. Many sites will support the new crowdfunding option, such as FundersClub, AngelList, EquityNet, Wefunder, and StartupValley. Equity crowdfunding comes with regulations on startups, such as reviewed or audited financial statements, background checks on executives, and an annual report to the SEC, which are not mandatory for angel or venture funding. Crowdfunding is a big opportunity, a big challenge, and still a big unknown.

- *Accelerators:* In the past five years, there has been a startup accelerator boom. But some of the first startup accelerators, such as the AOL Greenhouse, which launched Motley Fool and the Book Report Network, started long ago in the late 1990s, as playgrounds for innovation at big companies.

What is an accelerator today? A startup accelerator offers entrepreneurs a chance to spend a few months intensely focused on their product and business—fueled by funding and mentorship and often in shared office space—before pitching in front of investors at demo day. Most accelerators offer between $15,000 and $20,000, but some programs offer a convertible note on top of that.

The recent startup accelerator trend started with Y Combinator, founded by Paul Graham, Robert Morris, Trevor Blackwell, and Jessica Livingston. In 2007, David Cohen and Brad Feld founded Techstars in Boulder, Colorado, putting the city on the startup map as a place incubating and funding early-stage startups. The Techstars program has since expanded into a number of cities and niche verticals, and hundreds of other startup accelerators have emerged.

For more information on choosing the best startup accelerator, read Tech Cocktail's Guide to Startup Accelerators (see http://tech.co/book).

> ## Paul Graham
>
> Paul Graham is the cofounder of Y Combinator (2005), the first and now most prestigious startup accelerator. Silicon Valley–based Y Combinator has funded more than 450 startups, and more than 100 other startup accelerators have sprung up in its wake. Graham was a Lisp programming language expert and the cofounder of Viaweb (acquired by Yahoo! in 1998), which is claimed to be the first software as a service company. He writes well-regarded essays on startups at PaulGraham.com.

- *Hybrid programs:* A few organizations are adopting a hybrid model that has some similarities to an accelerator: funding, mentorship, and office space, without the demo day. Bloomington, Indiana–based SproutBox, for example, provides some minimal funding to startups in exchange for equity and mentors them over 10 months. Accepted companies start the program at different times during the year.

Los Angeles's Science Inc. is a technology studio led by former AOL and MySpace executives Michael Jones, Mike Macadaan, Peter Pham, and Ryan Sit, among others. Science Inc. funds ideas or develops them in-house and then applies its team of specialists to kickstart the company. It has worked with about 20 companies so far, including Dollar Shave Club and OUYA.

• *Startup competitions:* There are a number of startup competitions out there for you to take part in, such as MassChallenge in Boston, Challenge Cup in DC, Disrupt in San Francisco and New York, LAUNCH Festival in San Francisco, Women 2.0, and others that I've mentioned in previous chapters. You usually have to submit an application (often with a fee) and then compete on stage for prize money. That means you could get in but still end up earning no money. On the plus side, that money is *generally* equity free. There are plenty more out there for you to uncover and participate in—check out the list of popular startup competitions at http://tech.co/book.

How to Pitch to Investors

So you've made the decision you need investment and it's time to get out there and talk to investors. How are you going to present your idea and company? That is, what's your pitch going to be?

You usually do a presentation with slides (around 10 to 25) and include the who, what, why, and how of your business. But the pitch should be different depending on whom you're pitching to. Aziz Gilani, director of the Mercury Fund, explains, "Know your audience. Different investors want to see different things; some care about pedigree, while others care about technical details, while others care most about market traction. Cater your pitch to the things they care about."

Here are some elements of the pitch to consider including.

- *Problem and solution:* Show that the problem you're trying to address is a real issue. Be sure to explain who has this problem—in other words, explain who your customers are. Share how your solution solves this problem. But don't go into extreme detail. Your investors aren't your target customers. They just need to know you have a strong business and a sound value proposition.

- *Business model:* Explain your business model and how you'll make money. Reid Hoffman, cofounder of LinkedIn, believes it's best to talk about only one revenue stream; otherwise, investors will think you lack focus. I can't tell you how many times I've heard a pitch where the startup outlined three, four, or five possible revenue streams. Pick one—it's okay to be wrong and adjust it later. Share with your potential investors how you'll reach and acquire customers under that business model.

> ### Reid Hoffman
> Reid Hoffman cofounded LinkedIn in 2002, and it has since grown into the most popular business social network, with more than 200 million members as of January 2013. Hoffman's role has transitioned from CEO to chairman and president and now to executive chairman. He's also a partner at Greylock Partners, a Silicon Valley VC firm, and coauthor of the book *The Start-up of You*.

Also show how you'll use the funding you're looking to raise. It's helpful to include a timeline.

- *Metrics:* Share some metrics. Focus on bottom-up metrics such as revenue, engagement, and traction rather than top-down metrics such as total addressable market. Show that the cost of acquiring a customer is less than the lifetime value of a customer.

- *Challenges:* You'll want to address the challenges that your startup faces. Sharing your risks and challenges may be scary, but it has the reverse effect—it gives you more credibility by showing you think long term and tackle things head-on. For example, acknowledge that you have competition and explain why you're different and what advantages you have over them.

Jessica Kim, the cofounder of BabbaCo, raised funding while pregnant. She was originally shy and apologetic about it, and investors doubted her. Over time, she learned to be up front and tell investors how she was going to handle it before they even asked. This changed the conversation from doubts to confidence in her ability to execute. "Own it. You have to own it. If you feel confident and you're in control of it, investors (or suppliers or whoever you're going to partner with or people you're going to hire) are going to accept it more," Kim explains.

- *Team:* Your pitch is also about you and your team. In fact, your team may be even more important than your idea since the idea may change, and investors are investing in people. Share your qualifications; show expert knowledge of your industry and how you're the ideal people to build this business. Remember that you're pitching yourself throughout the interaction, including how confident and knowledgeable you appear and how you treat the investors.

Jeff Clavier of SoftTechVC is famous for this three asses rule. As an investor, he's looking for "a smart-ass team building a kick-ass product in a big-ass market." You'll find this rule on the back of Clavier's business card, on his website, in a painting in his office, and in the book *Do More Faster* by Brad Feld and David Cohen. But for SoftTechVC, the smart-ass team accounts for more than half the importance. SoftTechVC is open to funding multiple or solo founders, but it wants to see teams who exhibit the three Ds:

Jeff Clavier

Born in France, Jeff Clavier moved to Silicon Valley in 2000 to work with RVC, the venture fund affiliated with Reuters. (Reuters had acquired the startup he had been working on as chief technology officer.) Clavier left RVC in 2004 to found SoftTechVC and become a super angel, making larger investments than most angels. SoftTechVC gained attention and eventually raised its own fund, pioneering the micro-VC category. Since 2004, SoftTech has made more than 150 investments, including investments in Mint, Fitbit, and Eventbrite.

- Developer: Strong technical talent
- Design: An eye for user experience
- Distribution: Understanding of the tricks and rules of getting users

In the end, finding a smart-ass team is really a question of judgment. "It's a mix of vision, it's tenacity, it's empathy," says Clavier. "Do we feel that they have the passion, the domain knowledge, this unfair advantage that will make them execute and realize the potential of the company in a different way than the rest of the market?" He adds, "We really respect people who have this belief that if there is a wall, they can walk through it."

- *Fit:* Finally, as much as the pitch is about you, your team, and your startup, it's also a way to share why you fit with this investor. Feld likes to see pitches that include how you fit into his portfolio and expertise, and how you might be able to work with other portfolio companies. It shows that you did your research.

On your end, use every pitch as a way to gauge if you *do* fit with this potential investor. Sometimes you think you do, but you discover in a meeting that your styles of thinking or communicating conflict. If that's the case, you may want to find another investor that you mesh with better. You don't want your startup in bed with someone you don't jive with, so use your gut and go with what feels right.

"Ask to speak to entrepreneurs the VC has backed that have found success and those that haven't. Strive to understand in detail how the VC works with entrepreneurs in the good times and the bad and what the firm provides outside of the check. The good VCs want you to do this homework," says Eric Olson of Origin Ventures.

How Much Funding Should You Raise?

Figuring out your funding needs starts with a plan and budget. You need to map out what your growth plan looks like to get you to the next milestone or two, at which point you'll be able to raise more money or get acquired. Factor in estimates on how many employees you'll need, their costs, and other business costs and then determine the amount of money it'll take.

Graham offers this simple formula for determining your funding: multiply the number of people you want to hire times $15,000 times 18 (months). Version One Ventures founder Boris Wertz says you should aim for 15 to 25 percent dilution per round.

When raising seed funding, Dixon advises you to raise enough to get you to a Series A round with double the valuation (from postseed to pre–Series A), plus a fudge factor. What is the fudge factor? It's up to 50 percent more money to account for unexpected setbacks. As I mentioned earlier, you can't foresee every obstacle, and we're generally bad estimators of our time.

Funding will always be a delicate balance of raising too little and raising too much, and you probably won't get it right. When Jessica Mah was fund-raising for inDinero, the expense she didn't take into account was something she calls founder tuition. In a Stanford interview, she said that she wasted half of her initial $1 million in angel funding on her own mistakes. If she had to do it all over, she would have raised more.

In the summer of 2012 and into the spring of 2013, we saw new opportunities in downtown Vegas in the way of funding, partnership, and a bigger mission for Tech Cocktail. After just two visits, something clicked into place for us and we knew that working with the Downtown Project was the right move. So we relocated the company headquarters to Vegas and raised $2.5 million from the Downtown Project.

Here was a huge opportunity to apply our community building experience from Chicago, DC, Boston, and the many other cities we were privileged to get to know. We could help build a fresh tech startup community in Las Vegas—while continuing to scale our events and editorial coverage across the United States and eventually the globe.

It wasn't just about the funding, but the whole package that downtown Las Vegas had to offer. When I looked out across the vast empty parking lots from one of the top floors of the Vegas building that would soon be my home and Tech Cocktail's home, I saw a blank canvas. As an entrepreneur, I thought this was exciting and like no other opportunity I had seen before.

Fund-raising Tips

As in all areas of startup life, relationships matter when fund-raising. You want to get introductions to target investors from your other investors, from the target's portfolio companies, or from other mutual contacts. It makes sense to start building those relationships long before you're ready to raise money. As the common wisdom goes: ask for advice first, not money. Then, once you've made some progress along your path, come back with an update; if they like it, they may invest.

Research your target investors to understand what deals they like to do, then include that information in the fit section of your pitch. Look at their track record and what evidence of success they get excited about. For example, if you did some research on angel investor Esther Dyson, you'd find out that she isn't interested in a cute little app. She looks for companies solving big problems—problems that might not get solved by someone else. She wants to see founders with ambition and a spirit of adventure, but no grandiosity. If you don't do your research, you might waste her time—and yours.

Esther Dyson

Esther Dyson is an angel investor and a supporter of the health and space industries. She's the director of 23andMe, Russia's Yandex, and Meetup and has invested in companies such as Square and Flickr. Now, Dyson is devoting her attention to an initiative called HICCup, which would create citywide health intervention programs around preventive medicine, nutrition, and exercise. With a background in journalism, Dyson also serves on the board of various nonprofits.

And it's easy to waste time during the fund-raising process. This is one of the biggest issues that Graham warns against. He advises that only one founder focus on fund-raising so the whole company doesn't get derailed. He also says you shouldn't talk to investors who won't lead funding rounds. As for the rest, you can calculate how much time to devote to any one investor based on that person's expected value, which equals his or her probability of investing times the value of having the person as an investor. The more likely the person is to invest or the more valuable, Graham says, the more time you should devote to e-mailing, meeting with, and convincing him or her.

Keep in mind investor psychology. Basically, investors follow other investors, and they're motivated by not missing out on a big deal. You'll succeed according to how much momentum and competition you create: give off the vibe that this is a hot deal, and the investor better get in on it soon. The worst thing is to appear as if you've been out unsuccessfully fund-raising for a while and the deal is getting stale. According to Chris Schultz of Voodoo Ventures, "The best deals and founders always have a sense of urgency and momentum. You know they are going to close; its just a question of who and when … If you're out there 'kind of raising,' you are going to lose heat fast. It's all about momentum."

Once you get investors to say yes, be prepared for due diligence. It may be more or less comprehensive, but they generally want to investigate the soundness of your business before investing (including talking to customers, verifying finances, reviewing business plans, and more). Think of it like an inspection when you buy real estate: there are a number of things that could hold up the transaction, from a leaky roof to lead paint to a bug infestation. The same is true with startup funding.

To prepare for due diligence, make sure you have your intellectual property locked down if you come from a large corporation or hired independent contractors. Basically, everything we discussed in Chapter 4 on formation comes to the fore when you're out raising money. Anything you didn't do properly in the beginning can slow down your funding.

For a deeper dive on this topic, I highly recommend *Venture Deals* by Brad Feld and Jason Mendelson. For a list of tools for raising funding, check out http://tech.co/book.

The Harsh Reality

Raising a round of funding isn't easy. If it were, many more startups would do it. You're sure to encounter obstacles along the way. It's hard and can take lots of focus and time. Hoffman, in a detailed blog post about his Series B pitch to VC firm Greylock Partners (where he's now a partner), shares, "In a single year, the classic general partner in a venture firm is exposed to around 5,000 pitches; decides to look more closely at 600 to 800 of them; and ends up doing between 0 and 2 deals." Hoffman's post shares the odds pretty clearly with you—VC funding is not for everyone.

Evan Nisselson, an investor at LDV Capital, says, "It takes a long time, and you're going to get a lot of nos. So really it's a percentage game. If you don't have relationships with investors, you're probably going to have to meet 100 of them and hope one says yes." As Robin Chase recounts, even Zipcar had trouble raising funding. Investors were convinced that the car-sharing model worked great in Europe but wouldn't work in America.

Zipcar eventually got its funding, but your startup might not. You can lose focus on your day-to-day operations by going out and pitching to hundreds of investors. And hearing *no* more than you

> ### Robin Chase
>
> Robin Chase is best known as the founder of Zipcar, a car-sharing service that was launched in 2000. Zipcar expanded to more than 25 major metropolitan markets and hundreds of thousands of members and was acquired by Avis in January 2013. In 2011, Chase founded the peer-to-peer car-sharing marketplace Buzzcar in France, which reached more than 200,000 users in May 2013. A transportation enthusiast, she founded two other companies in between: GoLoco, a ride-sharing social network, and the transportation consulting company Meadow Networks.

hear *yes* could play tricks on your psyche if you start to question whether your idea is worth funding.

Fund-raising is a negotiation, and investors' and entrepreneurs' interests aren't always aligned. Investors don't mind if the process takes a lot of time, whereas entrepreneurs want to speed it up to keep the distraction as short-lived as possible—and get back to building their business. You might think things are moving along with an investor or group of investors, but the answer isn't yes until the papers are signed and the money is in the bank.

Finally, even if you have a great lawyer, investors may try to include terms that you don't like. Gilani recalls two entrepreneurs who turned down his funding offer in favor of a higher valuation. "Unfortunately for the entrepreneurs, the higher term sheet came with a management team and alternate vision for the company. Both founders were quickly replaced," he recounts.

Celebrate: Enjoy the Journey

Raising funding is not for everyone and in some cases isn't necessary. Ideally you would bootstrap until profitable or until an exit. But if you do decide to raise funding and do so successfully, you'll probably feel like you've been through a battle. You may want to have a little fun and celebrate before diving back into business. And we wouldn't blame you.

After two of Gilani's companies raised their funding rounds, they took the management teams on weekend camping trips to bond and plan milestones. I love the blend of work and play this example shows. They took a moment to celebrate but also to focus on the future and start the planning to go after it.

Many people believe that funding isn't a reason for celebration but rather a time to intensify the hustle. Funding is just a means to help you get where you want to go, you might think, so stopping to celebrate is premature.

But celebrating funding doesn't mean that you've made it and can relax. You can celebrate to commemorate all the hard work you put into the fund-raising process and to pause before digging in again harder than ever. I suggest you do this, for your own sanity. Starting and running a company is hard. If you don't enjoy the journey, then why are you doing it?

When Tech Cocktail finally closed our funding, we cracked open some bubbly for an after-hours celebration. I'd also been growing what I called the startup beard the entire time I was raising funding, an homage to the rally beards that you see in professional baseball, football, and hockey. Call it superstition or just a little crazy, but I didn't shave for the duration of the process—it was a constant reminder of the mission on hand: *close the funding*. My team and the community rallied around the startup beard, and there was even a #StartupBeard hashtag that started on Twitter and Instagram. Other entrepreneurs also shared their startup beards for me to see. After completing the funding round, I got to enjoy another celebratory moment when shaving my beard (which my significant other appreciated).

(I also grew a startup beard while writing this book and didn't shave it until a full draft was done. Seemed to work—if you're male, maybe you should try it. For more on the startup beard, check out http://tech.co/book).

Final Thoughts

Raising outside funding is not the right move for every company. Some companies can bootstrap to profitability and are never inclined to take on additional funds. For those that do raise funding, it can be a distracting, long, and lonely road. But you will learn a lot along the way, and hopefully this chapter helped lay some initial groundwork to get you started—we can't all raise funding in six days like Postling.

After raising funding at SXSW, Postling didn't go out and celebrate. The team kept improving the product and gained additional traction, which helped them raise another $350,000 the following year thanks again (in part) to AngelList. Two years later, they were acquired by LocalVox Media for an undisclosed amount—and hopefully they celebrated then.

Part 6
Growth and Change

16 Failure

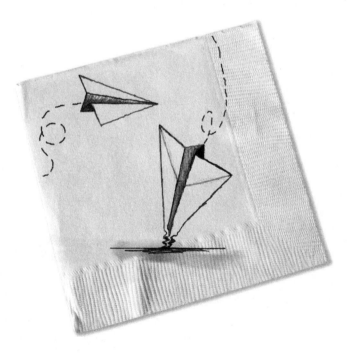

You build on failure. You use it as a stepping-stone. Close the door on the past. You don't try to forget the mistakes, but you don't dwell on it. You don't let it have any of your energy, or any of your time, or any of your space.

—Johnny Cash

After three years and $325,000 in funding from angels, friends, and family, Tara Hunt knew it was time. She had dreamed of building Buyosphere into the destination to find fashion from real people, but her dream hadn't taken flight. She and her team had to get new jobs.

"My dream was dashed. I was broke. I felt like a joke. I disappointed the friends and family who had invested in me. I didn't know what I wanted to do with my life anymore. I hadn't made a fallback plan," she writes.

Hunt had lost her identity. She became somewhat of a recluse, because all her old friends and old haunts reminded her of her pain and failure.

"I felt numb. I was in a state of numb for six months. I tuned out everything. I didn't want to hear about struggle or success or anything that was going on in the startup world or tech community. I unsubscribed from everything—every group, every list, every newsletter. I stopped talking to people who mattered in my life during my startup/tech days," she recalls.

And her new job didn't help. She picked up a low-paying one that she ended up hating, and they fired her after the trial period—as if her self-confidence weren't low enough already.

Hunt's failure is the kind of real, brave, honest story that you don't hear that often. That's ironic, because the startup world actually celebrates failure. Maxims such as fail fast, fail forward, and fail often have become gospel. Silicon Valley's FailCon is an annual conference to learn from other entrepreneurs' failures, and it also hosts informal FailChat meetups. Graphicly chief executive officer (CEO) Micah Baldwin says, "Failure is something that in America we love ... the [startup] process is a series of consistent and constant failure."

This chapter is about both kinds of failure—those failures along the way that we routinely talk about and those more lasting failures that we don't. The goals are to tell it like it is so you know what to expect and offer a few thoughts on how to weather the storm.

Divya Nag's failure story has a more positive outcome. After dropping out of Stanford her sophomore year, she started a company called Stem Cell Theranostics. She and her team had developed a technology to take stem cells; turn them into other types of cells, such as actual beating heart cells; and test drugs on them (without harming humans).

"I was so bright-eyed, I thought we were going to change the world," she recalls. "I figured if I can take skin and turn it into a heart cell, how hard could it be to commercialize this? Well, very famous last words. We decided to start the company, and that's when shit hit the fan."

Her first big lesson was that scientists are not cut out to be startup founders—not if they follow the traditional culture of the scientific community anyway. As a scientist, she says, you don't really share your failures or your methodologies. To gain recognition, you have to be the first one to publish positive results. The ones who keep their secrets the best are the ones who get published in top publications and get top research grants, further building a culture of secrecy.

One year after starting up, Stem Cell Theranostics had made no progress and hadn't had any commercial success. They were failing. Yet Nag noticed that her peers in the tech industry were succeeding—they had users and money. Why?

The answer was culture. Tech startups embraced failure and shared with each other openly, and that inspired Nag. She knew the medical industry—and Stem Cell Theranostics—had to change if they were going to succeed.

So Nag started StartX Med, part of the Stanford accelerator program StartX, to help medical entrepreneurs deal with all the challenges they face. The first thing she did was sit the medical entrepreneurs down next to the consumer information technology (IT) and hardware entrepreneurs, not allowing any two medical companies to sit next to each other. As techies complained about their bugs and problems, medical founders noticed, and they eventually opened up about their own.

That's when Stem Cell Theranostics turned around. They raised more than $20 million in funding (from grants) without giving up any equity, signed on three revenue-generating customers, got an exclusive license to their technology, and are now raising a $6.5 million seed round. And they have a viable product even though they're less than two years old—which might be nothing for a tech startup but is impressive in the medical industry. When they learned to embrace failure, they found success.

When Do You Shut Down?

Nag could have shut down Stem Cell Theranostics when the team ran into trouble, but she didn't. How do you know when to persist and when to give up?

Sean Percival was the cofounder and CEO of Wittlebee, which offered subscription boxes of kid's clothes. He eventually stepped down because they had a cash flow issue (they were on track for $3 million in sales but weren't yet profitable) and he was starting to lose his drive and passion.

In the last quarter of 2012, Percival had tried to push through a Series A round. But investors just weren't interested: Wittlebee was in the unpopular industry of subscription commerce for families. It was running low on cash and had cut staff, and things looked bleak.

Percival created a parody Twitter account called @SeriesACrunch to vent, with tweets such as "Andreessen passed on us but they did invest in a message board for rap lyrics. Now I've got 99 problems and apparently a pitch is one." That was one of his coping strategies, but the burden was just too much.

"My personal spirit and energy took a massive hit, from which I frankly never fully recovered," he says in a post called "How to Survive the Series A Crunch—From Someone Who Didn't." "It was the stressful on-again, off-again nature of our fund-raising that took a huge toll. The ups and downs can become so extreme in some cases that [it] quickly becomes unhealthy."

Percival was self-aware enough to realize that it was time to move on. But it's not always easy. The entrepreneurial instinct is to persist past obstacles and be optimistic, and it takes a lot of guts to admit that you've reached the end.

"It's great to be on a journey to make your career with your startup, but it's not always worth it," says Simon Lightstone, who shut down a microblogging tool called Snipia that he cofounded with his cousin. "Often, it's not just the founder who is making sacrifices. It's the founder's family, the employees who often need to slave away during hard times, and often others."

The Harsh Reality

You might think this whole chapter should be called "The Harsh Reality"—failure is the ultimate harsh reality of startup life. Hunt's experience gives you a hint about what it's like, but you won't know until you experience it.

When you fail, you have to admit it to your team and go about the process of firing your friends. You have to face family and friends, shut down your website, close your bank account and write an e-mail to your customers. You have to deal with all the credit card debt you've collected.

The list goes on. And you know you should do a postmortem so you can work through your thoughts and questions. Neal Cabage went so far as to write a book called *The Smarter Startup* as an exercise in reflection.

"After my second startup failed to get the traction I expected, I promised myself that I would not try another startup until I understood what went wrong and knew how to address it the next time," he recalls.

Those are the actions you take. But the feelings can be even more difficult. You wonder why you spent so much time on your startup; you regret the time you didn't spend with family and friends. You lose weight and sleep. You feel sad and probably angry, too.

"When CrowdRules folded, I was mad. I blamed my partner. I blamed customers and the market. I eventually got smart enough to blame myself. It was classic grieving—anger, denial, bargaining, depression, and finally acceptance and self-forgiveness. Self-forgiveness was *really* hard," says Tom Cox, cofounder of GrowthMaps.

People try to sympathize, as Hunt knows, but you aren't looking for sympathy. You don't want to keep telling the story over and over, trying to seem positive about it. You just want to be left alone with your feelings of stupidity, naivete, and low self-esteem.

"I dealt with some concerns that maybe I wasn't up to this kind of challenge, typical fears of inadequacy or incompetence," says Troy Davis, chief technology officer (CTO) of CoupSmart.

"I have personally had two startups fail; it hurts like nothing else. Without sounding disrespectful, I feel you can compare it with losing a loved one, and I feel comfortable making that comparison since I have experienced both myself. It's terrible. It makes you feel like a complete failure, and it can take months to process," says Robert Hoddenbagh, cofounder of MesaSix.

And finally, there's the cynicism. Your startup heart has been broken, and you can no longer go into another startup relationship with that bright-eyed, anything-is-possible mentality that only first-timers have. Words like *hustle* and stories of the latest million-dollar fundings will fall flat on your ears.

Ultimately, you'll have to decide if you want to do it again and risk another failure. And that may be the hardest decision of all.

How to Stay Positive

Learning how to stay positive despite failures along the way is the first step to learning how to deal with total startup failure.

According to behavioral scientist Matt Wallaert, who works at the search engine Bing, many entrepreneurs suffer from something called founder's disease. They don't talk to others enough about their failures, and that is emotionally draining and bad for business (after all, no one can offer support, connections, or advice if they don't know you're struggling). The solution, as Nag learned with Stem Cell Theranostics, is to start by being open about your troubles.

We can also look to psychology for some insight on dealing with setbacks, where we'll find support for the practice of self-compassion. One study showed that being compassionate toward yourself—rather than blaming yourself—makes you happy and less angry at the end of the day. And self-compassionate people actually take *more* responsibility than the self-blamers because they can admit their mistakes without feeling like an utter failure. If you're not naturally self-compassionate, you can induce self-compassion by writing a letter to yourself as if you were your friend.

Steve Corona, former CTO at TwitPic and author of *Scaling PHP*, stumbled upon a similar idea when he realized the importance of taking responsibility. "When you accept the blame, failure is easy. You aren't left with excuses, anger, and questions—the feelings are simple and the answer is obvious. It was all my fault. You can't blame anyone but yourself, and how can you possibly hold a grudge at *you*? It's easier to forgive yourself than it is to forgive others," he says.

Another psychological trick is positive reframing, or being able to see the benefits even in bad circumstances. It's a trait associated with self-esteem, optimism, and hardiness. And it's particularly useful for those who suffer from the doubts and worries of perfectionism. For example, you might try to focus on the lesson learned when your marketing flops or the helpful advice you got from a venture capitalist who rejected you.

One of the positive sides of failure is that it's a learning experience, a stepping-stone to success. A famous Nike commercial features basketball player Michael Jordan saying that all his failures—losing almost 300 games and missing more than 9,000 shots, 26 of which could have won the game for his team—are the reason he succeeds.

Twitter grew out of the failure of Odeo, a podcasting service. Groupon grew out of the failure of The Point, a site that allowed groups to organize and fund-raise for causes. In March 2012, Seesmic laid off half its staff and completely changed course, leading to an acquisition by HootSuite in September. These companies were able to succeed because they analyzed what was going on, salvaged what they could of their past work, and moved on.

Matt Galligan, a serial entrepreneur and now cofounder of Circa, says, "Accept failure. I think that we try so hard to sideline failure and just skip past it and be better than that, but the reality is you fail and you fail a lot and you have to just learn from those failures." At his early company SimpleGeo, their failure was trying to be too mainstream, which they wasted a year on. Once the company found its niche—powering the location features for app developers—things turned around.

Finally, for setbacks that can't be changed or remedied, acceptance is the right attitude. If you don't accept something—the flaws in your product or how late the release will be—you're basically in denial. And denying reality certainly won't equip you to handle it.

How to Stay Positive When Your Startup Fails

As you've grown your startup, maybe you've learned to not be too hard on yourself, look on the bright side, and accept reality. But if you're forced to shut down, all that will be put to the test.

Ellie Cachette was the founder of ConsumerBell, a startup that was improving consumer information related to recalls. At one point, she joked that they were like a cockroach that wouldn't die: despite their blog going down, having their credit line cut in half, and going through two suicides (their lead customer and their CTO's wife), the company was still alive. But in December 2013, Cachette and her team finally had to shut down.

Her response was one of gratitude and looking forward. "Of course I am sad, but I also know a ton of information and have ideas around areas that need my help, too," she wrote on the ConsumerBell blog. On her personal blog, she added, "After pouring hours of blood and tears and airport layovers and tough decisions, I can actually breathe for a minute and execute on other ideas and do it well … it's nice to know that I now have the time to do so. What a blessing." Now, Cachette is the vice president of product marketing at Koombea, a Web design and development agency.

Lightstone and his cousin, who had spent a year and a half and $35,000 on Snipia, finally gave up but managed to focus on what was even more important: their relationship. "After we officially decided not to pursue Snipia, my cousin and cofounder, then living in Israel, sent over a gift basket of beer and snacks to my place in Toronto. It was great. We loved each other anyways, but it was a sign that our connection was not hampered by the situation, and that life goes on," he says.

Brad Feld even recommends that startup communities hold wakes for failed entrepreneurs. This could be a dinner or a quiet evening out—anything to show them that failure is okay and their efforts didn't go unnoticed.

Feld knows something that you can come to realize after you go through a process of grieving. When your startup fails, your *startup* fails. You do not fail. That's true even if you decide that you won't try again—because you tried, and you made something, imperfect as it was. You tried, and you learned. You tried, and it's over, and there's nothing to do but be grateful for the opportunity and for all those who helped you. There's nothing to do but continue making yourself and your world better, because even if you don't have a startup anymore, you are an entrepreneur.

Final Thoughts

As for Hunt, she got through the failure by first finding a distraction: a job on a political campaign. Her candidate actually won, kickstarting the process of rebuilding her confidence.

"Slowly I had ideas. Inspiration. Drive. A desire to do something again. I slowly stopped feeling afraid. I slowly stopped feeling dread. I slowly regained confidence. I slowly stopped asking, 'Why would anyone want me?' and started believing in myself again," she says.

As of mid-2013, Hunt still wasn't back to her old self, but she felt "okay." She believes that you have to mourn, get some distance, and find your identity again when your startup fails. Now she's working with a partner on Lime Foundry, a social strategy agency, and Buyosphere is still running on the side.

"I can honestly say that I'm a much stronger, smarter, more interesting person for going through all of this," she writes. "And my next venture? It's going to be better for it."

> *Your self-worth has nothing to do with your craft or calling and everything to do with how you treat yourself.*
>
> —Kris Carr, Best-Selling Author and Wellness Activist

17 Success

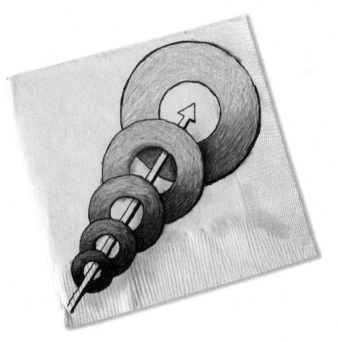

Growth is a spiral process, doubling back on itself, reassessing and regrouping.

—Julia Margaret Cameron

A t the mature age of 19, Matt Mullenweg founded WordPress. None of the other publishing platforms out there could do what he wanted, so he didn't just sit around and complain. He decided to build his own platform—scratch his own itch. It was a project fueled by passion.

Fast-forward to today, and Mullenweg is 30. The company he founded around WordPress, called Automattic, is celebrating its ninth birthday this year and has grown to about 230 team members. WordPress, the platform that started it all, is now powering about 21 percent of all websites.

Automattic has clearly reached product-market fit, and now the team is scaling. Scaling, also called the growth stage, comes after you've validated your idea and figured out the fundamentals of your business. You know people want what you have to offer, so it makes sense to push down on the gas pedal, ramp up your distribution, and grow! You spend money more quickly, but hopefully your revenues are growing even faster.

Mullenweg's first challenge was scaling the team—particularly because Automattic's culture is so democratic and flat. Most of the team works remotely, there are no set work hours, and employees can take as much vacation as they want. To make that work, Automattic takes the time to hire self-sufficient, passionate team members.

When Automattic hit 50 people, they split everyone into teams of five with a team lead, as author and management expert Scott Berkun recounts in the book *The Year without Pants*. These days, some teams at Automattic have up to 10 people. To ensure that everyone is collaborating, team leads who are working on the same project (like WordPress.com) get together and chat every few weeks.

Automattic has made about eight or nine acquisitions so far, which present their own challenges. To keep the company culture healthy, they mix up the new team with the old team. The companies they've added are never too big—less than 5 percent of the Automattic team, says Mullenweg—so they've never had a problem with clashing cultures.

Another interesting fact about Automattic is that the company barely uses e-mail. (Yes, I'm jealous.) Instead, they communicate on blogs called P2s, where they can post mockups, start discussions, and keep each other informed. That might not seem scalable, but Mullenweg insists it is. "This structure, I feel like could scale to 1,000 to 2,000 people before we had to have a major change," he says.

On the product side, Automattic is still figuring out how to evolve its processes as it grows. WordPress used to release a new version every six months, but Mullenweg realized that things were slowing down. So at the end of 2013, he and his team were experimenting with releases every two months. One of the dangers of scaling is slowed growth and innovation, and this is the tactic they're using to prevent that.

Your scaling experience will probably look different, but you'll have the same challenges: among them, growing your team, communication, and product releases. After that, you may be looking toward an exit. This chapter explains how to navigate the later stages of the startup journey.

Scaling

When exactly *do* you scale?

Unfortunately, it's not an exact science. The general strategy is to start scaling when you've hit product-market fit. That means that you've tested all your hypotheses about the business, your business model is sound, and people are giving you money. You know what your process for sales and customer acquisition looks like, and you're ready to start ramping it up. Recall that marketer Sean Ellis believes you've hit product-market fit when 40 percent of your users would be "very disappointed" if your product went away.

When you think it's time to scale, here are some of the elements to think about.

- *Human resources (HR):* Have you heard the saying "Don't work in the business; work on the business?" Well, now's the time to do that. If you're the chief executive officer (CEO), you should be extricating yourself from day-to-day operations and focusing more on strategy and overall direction. One area you might also devote your attention to is culture. The more people you hire, the higher the risk of your company culture derailing. As I mentioned earlier, if all the new hires understand the culture, they can make decisions faster without always having to ask for permission.

Mark Suster

Mark Suster is a Los Angeles–based serial entrepreneur turned venture capitalist. After selling two companies, he became a general partner at Upfront Ventures in 2007. He also founded the accelerator Launchpad LA and blogs about entrepreneurship at BothSidesOfTheTable.com.

Mark Suster of Upfront Ventures suggests that scaling companies hire an office administrator to relieve the CEO's duties and a vice president of finance to help with operations, legal, office space, board meetings, and fund-raising. Whomever you choose to hire, start keeping documentation of employee knowledge and processes—if someone leaves, you don't want the whole company to collapse.

- *Marketing:* Marketing in the scaling stage is about growth. It could include things such as testing different welcome e-mails, trying live chat on the website, making your tutorial shorter, or featuring testimonials. All these little tweaks can increase your conversions—and with a growing customer base, that could translate into real money.

    RJMetrics is a business intelligence tool that helps companies uncover insights from their data. While scaling, the company did something called a golden motion analysis, trying to figure out the one thing prospects do during a free trial that best predicts whether they'll sign up for the paid plan. For the RJMetrics software, the golden motion was creating a chart (because the chart helped customers see just how valuable the product was). So RJMetrics tweaked its free trial tours and training calls to highlight the chart editing tool, and conversion rates went up (to 89 percent in November 2013).

According to lean startup pioneer Eric Ries, there are three possible engines of growth for a startup. Can you tell which engine is driving yours?

- *Sticky:* Customers stick around for a long time. You want to focus on keeping them engaged.

- *Paid:* You grow by buying things, such as ads or real estate. You want to focus on raising revenue per customer or lowering customer acquisition costs. In other words, your challenge is to monetize better than your competition.

- *Viral:* Your customers advertise for you, or your product advertises itself. Early Hotmail spread to 11 million users in 18 months thanks to a tagline they added at Tim Draper's suggestion to the bottom of their e-mails: "Get your free email at Hotmail."

- *Product:* You may have found product-market fit, but you're not done learning. It's just that instead of pivoting, you're tweaking. You're optimizing the features you do have and testing new ones. The search engine Bing actually tested different

> **Tim Draper**
>
> Tim Draper is the founder and managing director of the venture capital firm Draper Fisher Jurvetson, which has funded companies such as Skype and Hotmail. He's also known as the creator of viral marketing: he suggested that Hotmail add a "Get your free email at Hotmail" line to the end of its e-mails, helping it spread to 11 million users in 18 months. Draper also launched the DFJ global network, with venture capital offices in more than 30 cities worldwide. And he recently announced the Draper University of Heroes, a boarding school in San Mateo to teach entrepreneurship to 18-to 24-year-olds. Draper is based in Silicon Valley.

shades of blue for its ad links and found that the right shade of blue brought in $80 million in additional revenue.

Scaling also means expanding into new markets. If you've been local, you may want to think nationally or internationally; if you've been niche, you may want to think mainstream.

- *Technical:* To prepare for growth, you want to make sure your technology can handle the increased load. This may be the time to scrap your code and start from scratch, if it wasn't properly built.

- *Metrics:* When you scale, different metrics start to matter. *Running Lean* author Ash Maurya believes you should transition from focusing on activation and retention to focusing on acquisition, revenue, and referral. In other words, you start getting more people to find out about your product, refer it to their friends, and pay for it.

  Rob Delwo, the vice president of operations at PivotDesk, has gone through the scaling process and has seen his focus shift from the product road map to sales and revenues. "In the growth stage, the company puts the majority of [its] effort on growing the top line, marketing and positioning, lead generation, converting customers in the pipeline, win rates, lowering churn rate," he explains.

- *Funding:* Even if you're profitable at this point, you may choose to take funding to ramp up your growth rate.

- *Operations:* Scaling means accelerating. You should look out for processes that your business does repeatedly and try to automate them.

- *Sales:* Your early salespeople had to be entrepreneurial, comfortable with the uncertainty of a constantly changing product and constantly changing methods of selling it. But now, you already understand how your customers acquire and use your product. If they fit with your team, more traditional salespeople could make good hires.

  Think of scaling like riding a bike. At first, before body-bike fit, you fall over a bunch of times. You try moving this way and that, leaning forward and backward, until you finally find your balance. Once you've learned the basic skill, you have a whole new set of skills to acquire: pedaling up hills and over potholes, racing with your friends, and navigating sharp turns. Get ready; now it's time to ride!

- *Partnerships:* As you grow, your startup gains influence and recognition—and value to other companies. Scaling may be the time to start thinking about forming mutually beneficial partnerships (if you haven't already). In Miami, for example, Tech Cocktail has teamed up with the Knight Foundation to shine a spotlight on all the exciting startup activity going on there. They offered us a grant, which in turn allowed us to expand our Miami coverage and hire a local writer and community manager. The fact that we had grown into a national platform made it a win-win for both sides.

> ## Knight Foundation
> The Knight Foundation supports innovations in journalism and media, engaged communities, and the arts through contests, grants, and funding. Their belief is that democracy thrives when communities are informed and engaged. Officially launched in 1950, the Knight Foundation was founded by brothers John S. and James L. Knight. The foundation's most famous initiatives include the Knight News Challenge, a $5 million international contest that funds innovations in news and information.

The Exit

If your ride is going well, you might find yourself on the path toward an exit. If you have investors, the exit is what returns their money to them (hopefully with interest), which is why they invested in you. For startups, an exit means either being acquired or doing an initial public offering (IPO). Exits aren't all unicorns and rainbows—during or after. But for many companies, they're the outcome you're shooting for. And if you pull it off, it can be the proud conclusion of your years of hard work.

Acquisitions are the much more common outcome, because IPOs are reserved for the best of the best. The legal fees for acquisitions are cheaper than IPOs, and you can expect the process to take a few months.

When you do decide to think seriously about an acquisition, you might hire someone in business development to start forming connections and relationships. That way, you could end up with several potential acquirers and a better negotiating position. According to Dan Martell, CEO and founder of Clarity, you should be connecting with the potential acquirer's CEO or founder, vice president of corporate development, and product manager.

As the initial discussions start, keep in mind the psychology of an acquisition. Buyers are always thinking: partner, build, or acquire? In other words, you have to convince them why buying you is more valuable than building the product in-house or just working with you.

In an IPO, you go from a private company to a public company. An IPO essentially functions like a fund-raising round: you sell shares of your company to the public to raise money. This process usually takes between 6 and 12 months. But going public is expensive and comes with a whole new set of regulations and Securities and Exchange Commission (SEC) reporting requirements. You won't see a payout as quickly thanks to regulations on when you can sell stock.

During the process, you work with an investment bank to sell shares in your company in the public market. Pricing the shares is always a balance between making money (pricing high) and generating demand and buzz (pricing low).

Should you aim for an exit? It makes no sense to plan to be acquired by Google or Facebook or Microsoft in x years. How can you predict what they'll want so far in the future? But you might generally decide whether you're looking for an acquisition, an IPO, or neither. That will give you a general direction, without tying you down to a plan that probably won't pan out.

The Harsh Reality

According to the Startup Genome Report, a study of more than 3,200 companies, 74 percent of high-growth Internet startups fail as a result of premature scaling. Scale too early, and you could be shooting yourself in the foot.

Scaling too early or incorrectly could mean spending too much money on customer acquisition, focusing too much on marketing and press, adding nice-to-have features before your core features are set, or hiring too many people. Startup Genome found that startups that scale too early have 20 times slower growth than startups that don't, raise less money in later rounds, and make less revenue per month.

LivingSocial cofounder Tim O'Shaughnessy knows the danger of scaling too early. "The perfect business is one that doesn't raise capital and is one that doesn't hire employees before it is operationally ready to, because the tax and the cost on that is really expensive," he says. He also knows that the scaling process is bumpy and complicated—and there are bound to be hiccups. "Things are not going to work and you're going to get frustrated by that," he says. "Be as up front as you can with your employee base about the fact that we're going to screw up ... When you scale, the likelihood of that occurring and somebody thinking that another group within the company is an idiot because they just don't know them as much anymore increases."

Even if you scale at the right time, you may find that your team members—who were so perfect for the scrappy startup stage—can't hack it in the growth stage. "Most people on founding teams aren't well equipped to go to the next level," says organizational psychologist Mike "Dr. Woody" Woodward. You may be forced to find another position for them or fire them altogether—and that includes the CEO.

WordPress had its own scaling challenges. In *The Year without Pants*, Berkun recounts his nearly two years at WordPress, where he was hired to lead a team and help the company navigate its new team-based structure. One of the issues he saw was a culture that favored making incremental improvements (fixing bugs) rather than focusing on the broad vision and user experience. As your startup scales and your employees become more specialized—not wearing so many hats—watch out for the phenomenon of "it's not my job."

Another challenge Berkun saw at WordPress was the culture around money. If you're a WordPress user, you might have noticed that it's hard to find the WordPress Store. Many WordPress programmers are used to doing work for free, Berkun writes, and making money isn't a huge emphasis there. The takeaway lesson is that scaling may mean you're no longer struggling to survive, but every employee should still understand his or her connection to the bottom line.

Perhaps the harshest scaling reality is not when you scale too early or have team troubles but when you discover that your product actually isn't scalable at all. The size of your market may not be big enough (experts recommend around $1 billion), or your costs may just be too high. Either way, it's your choice to continue running a business that won't achieve rocket ship growth—a perfectly respectable choice—or go back to the drawing board to pivot to an idea that is scalable.

Assuming you do survive until exit time, you have a whole new set of harsh realities to face. Even though you're almost at the end, you may be fighting an uphill battle, like TeRespondo did.

From 2003 to 2005, Google and Yahoo! were embroiled in an acquisition process with TeRespondo, the AdWords of Latin America. I say "embroiled," because it wasn't a friendly situation.

At one point, Google and Yahoo! were trying to poach TeRespondo's largest partner, UOL. So TeRespondo's CEO, Juan Diego Calle, did the only thing he could think of. "I remember chasing our partner—one guy in that company—around the West Coast from Mountain View all the way to Pasadena while he talked to our competitors, to Google and Yahoo!" recalls Calle. "I was chasing him from location to location—literally, I was after him from hotel to hotel—and making sure that at the end of the night after he was done having these conversations with my competitors, that I would end up having a drink with the guy at the bar."

Throughout the process, Calle says, Google and Yahoo! both tried to poach TeRespondo's employees, too. He worried that they were just showing interest in order to figure out what he was doing and then copy it. "We were defending ourselves from these two monsters trying to enter our market," he says. "It wasn't a friendly situation where you go present the company and everyone's happy and interested."

It was a long year and a half. Some months there was no activity whatsoever, and TeRespondo was torn over where to focus its energies— on getting the deal done or on running the company. Because it was a cash-strapped startup, management couldn't just hire someone to handle the deal for them. But TeRespondo survived. It had survived the dot-com crash, and it survived this—finally getting acquired by Yahoo! in 2005.

Even if your exit process is smoother than TeRespondo's, you may not feel total jubilation once it's over—for the same reason some parents tear up when their kids go to college: your identity is so tied up with being a founder. Entrepreneur Jason Cohen, now the CEO of WP Engine, sold a startup called Smart Bear and shared his feelings in a post called "Startup Identity & the Sadness of a Successful Exit." He writes, "Almost all startup founders experience a deep and prolonged sadness after selling their company, even when the sale is an outrageous success. Why? ... A startup founder lacks this distinction between personal identity and work identity ... A startup *is* the founder's personal identity."

And not every exit brings in a profit. Your friends may all be congratulating you on selling your company while you cringe inwardly because you didn't even return all the money to investors. Cofounder Mo Yehia, who sold a startup called Sqoot, writes, "We saw a seven-figure deal evaporate into thin air because we had no leverage. Buyers toyed with us like a great white [shark] toys with a seal prior to devouring it.

Ultimately, while most investors made nominal money, others lost big time."

Other times, you may stay at the acquirer only to see your product get used in a way you didn't expect. Once you sell, you no longer have full control. The acquirer may want to fold your product into theirs, get rid of your brand, or shut it down altogether. That's what happened to Gowalla, which was acquired by Facebook in December 2011 and shut down in March of the following year.

Celebrate: Enjoy the Journey

In the growth stage, you're still racing hard, but it's a great time to look back and see how far you've come. You've reached product-market fit, something that many startups don't achieve.

Be grateful that your team is getting bigger, which means that the group of people who believe in your vision is expanding. You can take off a few of your many hats and breathe, because it's time to delegate some responsibility to others.

"As a startup we had a small team that was always on the same page and shared a vision. Scaling requires adding more team members and other employees, getting them to buy into your vision and work toward achieving a common goal. This can be challenging but rewarding when it all comes together," says Hannah McConaghy, marketing coordinator at UberPrints.com.

Exits can be celebrated for a similar reason: you've found a group of people—a whole company, in fact—who believe in your vision. And, of course, you're finally being externally rewarded for the value you've created.

In *Startup Life*, Brad Feld and his wife, Amy Batchelor, recommend taking 10 percent of your earnings and splurging on something special to celebrate the moment. After that, wait 90 days to figure out what to do with your newly earned payout. It's easy to rush into a decision, when you really should be taking your time.

"You've worked incredibly hard to get to this point; figure out shared things and experiences that will be special to you. While they don't have to be tangible, the memories can be long lasting," they write.

Take a vacation, get some sleep, exercise, and say thank you to all the people who helped you along the way. It's their celebration, too.

Final Thoughts

Despite its challenges, Automattic has made sure to scale at least one thing incredibly well: its culture. They've always valued transparency, so bug fixes, features, and other changes are discussed out in the open. The founders shun hierarchy and bureaucracy in favor of meritocracy: job titles aren't important, and the people who get the most respect are those who create and contribute.

Unlike many founders, Mullenweg doesn't talk much about exiting. He believes in longevity: he sees WordPress as his life's work and would be happy working on it for years to come. And the product is deliberately set up that way: no matter what Automattic does to Word-Press, anyone can take the open source code and "fork" it to form a new version. WordPress will live on.

The most important lesson that Berkun took away from Automattic is that work doesn't have to be serious or meaningless. Automattic showed him a place where employees find passion and meaning, as well as humor and joy. And that is something that many new entrepreneurs discover.

CONCLUSION

This is the conclusion, but the learning doesn't have to end here—keep in touch with us at http://tech.co/book.

Parading down Las Vegas Boulevard with two llamas by my side, surrounded by conference attendees, startup founders, friends, relatives, and our Tech Cocktail team, I felt a sense of momentary relief, happiness, and accomplishment. We had just completed the first day of our Tech Cocktail Celebrate conference in downtown Las Vegas.

It was the culmination of a yearlong event schedule, as we toured the country in search of the hottest startups in every city we visited. The final stretch consisted of a 12-event road trip in the last month leading up to the big day. Then, my team surprised me with the llama parade to our evening festivities—they knew that I loved llamas and it would surely put a smile on my face, as well as our attendees'.

We were now less than 24 hours from crowning the hottest startup in the country, and all the months of preparations had come together. Although there were, of course, some hiccups along the way, we had persevered and learned a lot in the process. It was a big year: we had expanded our team and raised funding to accelerate toward our goals, and for that moment we felt on top of the world, while knowing this was just the beginning. We still had a future to look forward to as we continued to expand and grow.

Knowing the nature of the startup journey, I expected the roller coaster to race back down and even out soon enough. So with that in mind, I decided to be as present as possible, marveling in the llamas and just enjoying the ride (or parade) as it happened.

Starting a company is hard work. Will you face hardships? Probably. Will you work harder than you have in your whole life? Most likely. Will the reward be worth the frustration? Absolutely.

So get started on your startup adventure, armed with this mixology of startup ingredients to help you find your way. Here's to you!

Cheers,

Frank

ACKNOWLEDGMENTS

'd like to take a moment to say thank you to everyone who made this book and my startup life possible.

Thank you to my family and friends (in no particular order)—Jen, Paulette, Frank, Linda, John, Joe, Maureen, Jessica, Mike, Brittany, Mackenna, Ryan, Jack, Beverly, Charlie, Anne Marie, Tim, Audrey, Ben, David, Fran, Mia, John, Elliott, Jasper, Sam, and Wolfgang Wolfdog—for all your support and understanding throughout my startup journey and life. Thank you to my old friend John Guidos, who urged me to continue to pursue writing a book—let the good times roll!

Thank you to my amazing team, who worked tirelessly to make this book a reality. Merci to Kira M. Newman for being the compass that guided this project ahead. Your research helped infuse each chapter with a diverse and lively set of perspectives. You truly are an integral part of this book and our story, and I could not have done it without you—thank you!

Grazie to my loving wife and partner, Jen Consalvo. I'm grateful you joined me for this journey, for your years of support, and for bringing stories, perspective, knowledge, and a critical editing eye to bear throughout this process.

Gracias to my mom, Paulette, for jumping in to lend your editing skills and time to making sure this book passed the mom test.

Danke to Justin Thorp for helping brainstorm and act as a sounding board throughout the process, along with pour-over coffee—best seller or bust! To Mollie Andrade for shielding my schedule so I could crank on this book. To James Barcellano for making our Tech Cocktail technology hum for book readers. Thank you to our early employee Julia Fischer for believing in the vision before we had a team or funding to support it. Thank you to Zach Davis for contributing insights, stories, support, and long-bearded inspirations. Thank you to Tori Burroughs for all of the fabulous illustrations in this book. Thank you to the rest of our team: Kim Blackburn, Mary Ellen Delaney, Steve Kann, and everyone else, as well as the growing list of fabulous contributors.

Mahalo to the island of Kauai for a few rainy days and rainbows on my honeymoon, which enabled me to work on some chapters and not feel quite as guilty.

Thank you to Tech Cocktail's partners and supporters, including .CO, American Airlines, the Knight Foundation, AOL, Cars.com, Intel, Microsoft, the Kauffman Foundation, Startup Weekend, UP Global, 1776, iStrategyLabs, FR&R, Evan Brown, Saper Law, SingleHop, ChicagoMicro, Sprint, and the hundreds of others who have supported our efforts along the way.

Thank you to Eric Olson for teaming up with me back in Chicago in 2006 to bring Tech Cocktail to life, building a foundation, and continuing to support its growth along the way. Thank you for your hard work and dedication to get it off the ground. You were right; this could be big. Most important, thank you for your friendship. Of course, thank you to Laura, too, for putting up with our crazy ideas and long Tech Cocktail brainstorming sessions. And to Eric's family, including John, Carolyn, Laura B., Laura O., Jeff, Jack, and Caesar, thank you for your ongoing support.

Thank you to Brian Solis, Rohit Bhargava, Jenn Lim, Sarah Lacy, Paul Simon, Amy Jo Martin, and Matt Sitomer for your help, support, and book industry knowledge. Thank you to early blogosphere friends, including Michael Arrington, Om Malik, Richard MacManus, Orli Yakuel, Marshall Kirkpatrick, Gabe Rivera, Lee Odden, and many more.

Thank you to Tony Hsieh, Fred Mossler, and the Downtown Project for believing in Tech Cocktail and partnering with us.

Thank you to all the people in my life who have volunteered in some way—whether it was pouring wine, managing registration tables (especially our long-time Chicago bouncers Jess, Kelly, and Melissa, early Chicago and DC supporters and countless others), helping me with code, giving me a place to crash, or introducing me to someone else—I am eternally thankful. There are too many of you to list, which makes me even more appreciative and grateful.

Thank you to all of our Tech Cocktail nation. If you have ever read one of our articles or attended one of our events in any city, you know who you are. To all the Ron Mays of the world, you kept us on our toes. A glass tip to you—cheers!

Much love and gratitude to everyone who has ever supported and believed in me and my endeavors. You all played a part in this, and I thank you.

REFERENCES

Berkun, Scott. *The Year without Pants: WordPress.com and the Future of Work*. San Francisco, CA: Jossey-Bass, 2013.

Bhargava, Rohit. *Personality Not Included: Why Companies Lose Their Authenticity—And How Great Brands Get It Back*. New York: McGraw-Hill, 2008.

Blumberg, Matt. *Startup CEO: A Field Guide to Scaling Up Your Business*. Hoboken, NJ: Wiley, 2013.

Cachette, Ellie. "Goodbye from ConsumerBell (2013)," *ConsumerBell* (blog), November 2013, http://blog.consumerbell.com/2013/11/25/goodbye-from -consumerbell-2013/.

Cachette, Ellie. "I Shutdown My Startup Today," *Ellie Cachette* (blog), November 25, 2013, http://www.elliecachette.com/1/post/2013/11/i-shutdown-my-startup -today.html.

"Celebration." Startup America, accessed February 21, 2014, http://www.s.co /champions/training/celebration.

Chen, Andrew. "Growth Hacker Is the New VP of Marketing," *@andrewchen* (blog), April 27, 2012, http://andrewchen.co/2012/04/27/how-to-be-a-growth-hacker -an-airbnbcraigslist-case-study/.

Cohen, Jason. "Startup Identity & the Sadness of a Successful Exit," *A Smart Bear* (blog), February 26, 2013, http://blog.asmartbear.com/startup-identity-selling -sadness.html.

Dao, Francisco. "Tech Community: Are We MTV or TED?" *Washington Post*, August 19, 2011, http://www.washingtonpost.com/national/on-innovations /tech-community-are-we-mtv-or-ted/2011/08/18/gIQASfGsNJ_story.html.

Davis, Zach. *Appalachian Trials: A Psychological and Emotional Guide to Successfully Thru-Hiking the Appalachian Trail*. Boulder, CO: Zach Davis, 2012.

Dixon, Chris. "Firing," *Chris Dixon* (blog), June 19, 2012, http://cdixon.org/2012 /06/19/firing/.

Feld, Brad. *Startup Communities: Building an Entrepreneurial Ecosystem in Your City*. Hoboken, NJ: Wiley, 2012.

Feld, Brad, and Amy Batchelor. *Startup Life: Surviving and Thriving in a Relationship with an Entrepreneur*. Hoboken, NJ: Wiley, 2013.

Feld, Brad, and Mahendra Ramsinghani. *Startup Boards: Getting the Most out of Your Board of Directors*. Hoboken, NJ: Wiley, 2014.

Gil, Elad. "Never Ever Compromise: Hiring for Culture Fit," *Elad Blog* (blog), April 12, 2012, http://blog.eladgil.com/2012/04/never-ever-compromise-hiring-for .html.

Godin, Seth. *Purple Cow: Transform Your Business by Being Remarkable*. New York: Penguin, 2003.

Hoffman, Reid. "LinkedIn's Series B Pitch to Greylock: Pitch Advice for Entrepreneurs," *Reid Hoffman* (blog), accessed February 21, 2014, http://reid hoffman.org/linkedin-pitch-to-greylock/.

Hoffman, Reid. "What I Wish I Knew Before Pitching LinkedIn to VCs," LinkedIn, October 15, 2013, www.linkedin.com/today/post/article/20131015161834-12 13-what-i-wish-i-knew-before-pitching-linkedin-to-vcs.

Hsieh, Tony. *Delivering Happiness: A Path to Profits, Passion, and Purpose*. New York: Business Plus, 2010.

Hunt, Tara. "The End of My World as I Knew It and I (Now) Feel Fine... [A Retrospective on Startup Grief]," *Tara Hunt* (blog), June 27, 2013, http:// tarahunt.com/2013/06/27/startup-grief/.

Mah, Jessica. "A Startup Is a Learning Experience," interview at Stanford University's Entrepreneurial Thought Leaders Lecture Series, Stanford, CA, November 30, 2011.

Marmer, Max, Bjoern Lasse Herrmann, Ertan Dogrultan, and Ron Berman. *Startup Genome Report Extra on Premature Scaling*. San Francisco, CA: Startup Compass, 2011.

Martin, Amy Jo. *Renegades Write the Rules: How the Digital Royalty Use Social Media to INNOVATE*. San Francisco, CA: Jossey-Bass, 2012.

McClure, Dave. "Startup Metrics for Pirates: AARRR!!!" SlideShare, August 8, 2007, http://www.slideshare.net/dmc500hats/startup-metrics-for-pirates-long-version.

Moore, Geoffrey. *Crossing the Chasm: Marketing and Selling High-Tech Products to Mainstream Customers*. New York: HarperCollins, 1991.

Percival, Sean. "How to Survive the Series A Crunch—From Someone Who Didn't," *Sean Percival* (blog), June 3, 2013, http://www.seanpercival.com/blog/2013/06/03/how-to-survive-the-series-a-crunch-from-someone-who-didnt/.

Roberts, Jason. "How to Increase Your Luck Surface Area," Codus Operandi, 2010, http://www.codusoperandi.com/posts/increasing-your-luck-surface-area.

Sinek, Simon. "How Great Leaders Inspire Action," TEDx Puget Sound, Puget Sound, WA, September 2009.

Taub, Alexander. "How We Launched a Massive Product with 40+ Partners," Medium, October 29, 2013, https://medium.com/on-startups/eed2cfaf352d.

Taub, Alexander. "What I've Been Working on for the Past 11+ Months," *Alex's Tech Thoughts* (blog), October 2013, http://alexstechthoughts.com/post/64770552391/what-ive-been-working-on-for-the-past-11-months.

Wilson, Fred. "Overcommunicating?" *AVC* (blog), April 27, 2006, http://avc.com/a_vc/2006/04/overcommunicati.html.

Yehia, Mo. "Sell Your Company, Not Your Soul," *Me llamo Mo* (blog), August 8, 2013, http://moyehia.com/post/57730952805/sell-your-company-not-your-soul.

INDEX